# FOREST CATS

## of NORTH AMERICA

Cougars
Bobcats
Lynx

JERRY KOBALENKO

PHOTOGRAPHY BY
THOMAS KITCHIN
& VICTORIA HURST

FIREFLY BOOKS

# A FIREFLY BOOK

**Cataloguing-in-Publication Data**

Kobalenko, Jerry
    Forest cats of North America

ISBN 1-55209-172-4

1. Pumas.    2. Bobcat.    3. Lynx.
I. Kitchin, Thomas (Thomas W.).
II. Hurst, Victoria (Victoria N.).
III. Title.

QL737.C23K62   1997    599.75'3    C97-930888-7

Published by
Firefly Books Ltd.
3680 Victoria Park Avenue
Willowdale, Ontario
Canada M2H 3K1

Published in the U.S. by
Firefly Books (U.S.) Inc.
P.O. Box 1338, Ellicott Station
Buffalo, New York 14205

Produced by
Bookmakers Press Inc.
12 Pine Street
Kingston, Ontario K7K 1W1

Design by
Ulrike Bender
Studio Eye

Cartography by Roberta Cooke

Color separations by
Friesens
Altona, Manitoba

Printed and bound in Canada by
Friesens
Altona, Manitoba

Printed on acid-free paper

# CONTENTS

4    Introduction

8    **Chapter 1: THE LEGEND, THE SURVIVOR AND THE INTROVERT**
     8    The Legend: The Cougar
     12    Cougar Science
     17    The Kitten and the Killer
     22    The Survivor: The Bobcat
     22    Forever Rivals
     26    Facts and Fantasies
     30    The Introvert: The Lynx

38    **Chapter 2: BONES OF CONTENTION**
     41    The Two "C's"
     43    The Chicken or the Egg?

48    **Chapter 3: ON THE PROWL**
     50    Feast or Famine
     50    A Dangerous Profession
     52    The Predator-in-Chief
     54    Misunderstandings
     56    The Lynx and the Hare: A Classic Cycle Revisited
     59    Snapping the Cycle
     62    The Cycling Bobcat?
     63    Two Kills Witnessed

68    **Chapter 4: BRIEF ENCOUNTERS**

80    **Chapter 5: MAN AND CAT**
     80    First Contact
     83    The Furred Demon
     84    The Crime of Crimes
     89    Grand Attack Central

92    **Chapter 6: TWO MODERN CAT TALES**
     92    Florida Panther: The Glamour Puss
     94    The Old Florida
     96    Clones
     99    Eastern Cougar: A UFO With Paws
     100    The Case Against
     103    The Case For

110    **Chapter 7: FELINE FUTURES**

     118    Acknowledgments
     120    Sources
     125    Index

# BEAUTY AND THE BEAST

*But the wildest of all the wild animals was the Cat. He walked by himself, and all places were alike to him.*

—RUDYARD KIPLING, *JUST SO STORIES*

RUDYARD KIPLING'S TALE OF "THE CAT THAT WALKED BY Himself" hints at why we have admired and even worshiped the cat for 4,000 years. It is, first of all, a lovely animal. It lives everywhere, yet lightly, as if half not belonging. Flattering ourselves, we identify with its grace, its independence and its incorruptibly wild nature. We look at it and see the beauty and the beast within ourselves.

Cougars, bobcats and lynx take their cathood even further than most of the world's 37 feline species. They are not only beautiful; they are not only incorruptible; they are ghosts. Every year, I spend at least two months traveling the North American wilderness. I've seen plenty of wolves and bears. I've even seen a wolverine. But I've never seen a wild cat. I have no doubt, however, that *they* have seen me.

Overseas, big cats are much less elusive. In Botswana's Okavango Delta, I have seen lion cubs biting their mother's ears, a leopard vaulting into a tree and a cheetah scanning the scrub mopane forest from its termite-mound lookout. In Russia's Far East, I've walked in tiger tracks; and in Nepal's Chitwan National Park, I narrowly missed being one of the many visitors to see a tiger in the wild. Yet in North America, some people spend their entire lives in the

*Cougars need huge amounts of space, especially since agriculture and settlement claimed our most fertile valleys decades ago, forcing the cats to survive mainly in deserts and mountain fastnesses.*

bush and never see a cougar. A fleeting glimpse of one of these unsocial predators is often a pivotal moment in our lives, a connection with our primitive past and with the retreating wilderness of this continent.

Perhaps one day, I'll be lucky enough to watch a cougar pouring its way like liquid mercury over a Rocky Mountain slope or a gangly lynx picking its shy and careful way through Labrador's black-spruce forest. In the meantime, I've tried to satisfy my curiosity and affection by tracking cats in the jungles of big libraries and through the tangled brush of telephone lines across North America. It has been reassuring to discover along the way that many of the

*Blurred by a curtain of spruce boughs, a bobcat lies in wait for a passing rabbit. Despite their need for space, wild cats depend on their ability to hide for hours in claustrophobic little corners of the forest, waiting for unsuspecting prey.*

6

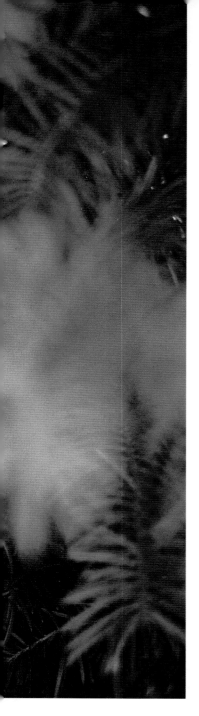

scientists who study wild cats full-time have also never seen one which has not been treed by dogs or caught in a trap or pinpointed by its radio-collar.

There is a downside to this elusiveness, of course. Our understanding of wild cats has been limited by the difficulty of studying them. Sometimes even the simplest questions—How many are there? How long have they been around?—represent monumental scientific puzzles. North American cats are so vehemently solitary, so intolerant of intrusion, that their very mystery can foster a lack of appreciation. No one has told them about the benefits of good public relations: Wild cats don't waddle like penguins or look chubby and endearing like pandas or howl like wolves on eerie summer nights. Wild cats don't want to know us. They don't want to be our wilderness kin. They're hermits.

Although we may never be able to share a meadow with wild cats, we can still marvel at what a tremendous evolutionary state these hypercarnivores have achieved. A bobcat may sit motionless on a hare trail for up to seven hours, waiting for its prey to appear. A 100-pound cougar can haul a 600-pound elk up a mountain in its jaws. In its tireless pursuit of a snowshoe hare, a lynx will float over foot-deep powder snow as if on wings. In the end, these secret sharers of our woods exist as masterpieces of creation, like a Fabergé egg or a Ferrari, things which most of us will never possess but which we can admire from afar.

# CHAPTER 1

# THE LEGEND, THE SURVIVOR AND THE INTROVERT

## THE LEGEND: THE COUGAR

MARTIN JALKOTZY IS LUCKIER THAN MOST OF US. OVER THE course of a 14-year cougar study in Alberta, the Calgary researcher had several remarkable glimpses into the life of this mystery cat. He has seen a cougar speeding after two mule deer, so light on its feet that it seemed not to be touching the ground, "yet it left paw marks." He has come upon a female squatting beside her prey just seconds after the kill, utterly spent, her chest heaving violently, her breath smoking in the frosty Rocky Mountain air. But on his most memorable sighting, Jalkotzy saw nothing.

It was in the foothills of the great peaks, in a region called Kananaskis Country, just outside Banff, Alberta. A skiff of snow covered the small spruce and aspen stand where Jalkotzy was tracking the recent passage of a cat. Cougars often wander from spruce to spruce, hoping to bump into deer or rabbits that bed down beneath the lowest boughs. "I was walking around my millionth spruce of the day," he recalls, "when all of a sudden, a cougar exploded from underneath it. I know it was a cougar, yet it moved so fast that I have no image in my mind of that cat. It was gone before my eyes could focus." That absence of a mental image left a deep impression on the researcher, who is a trained observer: The cougar had been less than three feet away.

Little wonder that the cougar is sometimes known as the phantom cat. But as befits an animal that ranges from the Yukon to Chile, the cougar has dozens of names—42

*Pursued by wolves, dogs or other enemies it can't outrun, a cougar will take to a tree and remain there for days, if it must. Safe in its perch, it may behave with lordly indifference to its pursuers. Cougars have been known to fall asleep on a limb with dogs barking frantically below.*

in English alone and hundreds more in Spanish, Portuguese and the many native languages. In North America, cougar, panther, puma and mountain lion are its most common names. Although "panther" is probably more widespread, I prefer "cougar" because of what it reveals about the cat. "Cougar" is derived from a Tupi word that means "false deer," which demonstrates that these ancient Amazonians may have had an instinctive understanding of a modern scientific idea: a predator evolves to blend into the same habitat as its chief prey. Even the subtle color differences between cougar populations seem to correspond to the shadings of the indigenous deer.

The cougar is truly a creature of superlatives. No mammal other than humans ranges as widely in the western hemisphere. None jumps as high. None hunts bigger prey for its size. And perhaps no mammal in North America has sex as often.

It's dangerous to draw conclusions about wild-animal behavior from captives, but in an effort to observe a cougar

*A wild cat is as fastidious as any house cat and spends long hours grooming away both the forest mud and all traces of its meals. Clean fur is not a luxury but is essential both as a protection against the cold and to minimize scent.*

# COUGAR BASICS

| | |
|---|---|
| Scientific name: | *Puma concolor* |
| Other common names: | puma, panther, catamount, mountain lion |
| Number of subspecies: | 29*; 10 in Canada and the United States |
| North American population: | 20,000 |
| Length with tail: | males, 11 feet; females, 8 feet |
| Weight: | males, 145-165 pounds; females, 75-100 pounds |
| Habitat: | anywhere there's cover, wilderness and ungulates |
| Size of territory: | 8-500 square miles |
| Diet: | mainly deer and elk; also hare, porcupine, raccoon, squirrel, rabbit, beaver, muskrat |
| Gestation: | 90-95 days |
| Size of litter: | 1-6; usually 2-3 |
| Birth weight of young: | 1 pound |
| Time with mother: | 18-24 months |
| Life span: | 8-11 years in the wild |

\* Not counting the probably extinct eastern cougar

up close, I made regular visits to the local zoo over the course of several months. The cougar there, a 10-year-old male, came to know me well enough to react when I appeared. Sometimes, he rolled on his back and purred like a lap cat. Sometimes, as I circled his enclosure, he shot out of nowhere in a mock attack. He was a curious mixture of kitten at heart and predator to the core.

The more I studied him, the more I became almost oppressively aware of his physical superiority. We both weighed about 160 pounds, and although I consider myself fairly fit, I felt awkward next to this fur-upholstered pack of muscles. "His daily routine is a march of stirring athletic events," wrote naturalist Ernest Thompson Seton almost 100 years ago. One Idaho researcher explained that in one or two bounds, a cougar could routinely descend cliffs which took his team of trackers entire hair-raising afternoons to negotiate. I recalled snippets I'd read and others I'd heard: about the Texan, for instance, who had hitched up a team of horses to drag away a dead 600-pound steer, only to discover that a cougar had already hauled it off...or the cougar that leapt 12 feet onto a ledge with a 165-pound buck in its jaws...or the cats which have hit an elk with such force that the elk's antlers were driven into the ground.

Before my firsthand observations of the captive cougar, I found it hard to believe that a small 55-pound animal could ever kill a human adult, as happened in 1996 in British Columbia when a mother died protecting her child from a cougar attack. But gradually, I began to understand. Here is an animal built for hitting much larger prey with the impact of a small truck. The cougar is literally armed to the teeth. Viselike jaws drive its 1½-inch dagger teeth. Five one-inch razor-sharp claws tip each sledgehammer paw. Add to this a fighting skill that surpasses any martial artist, a Ninja-like invisibility and reflexes twice as fast as those of Muhammad Ali in his prime. Suddenly, all those superlatives about the cougar—and Martin Jalkotzy's experience with the cat that wasn't there—started to make sense.

## COUGAR SCIENCE

Under pressure from either their government bosses or curious writers, biologists may admit that there are about 20,000 cougars in North America, including some 5,500 in California, 3,000 in Oregon, 3,800 in British Columbia and 800 to 1,000 in Alberta. But settling on population figures for the cougar is like guessing how many fish there are in the sea—no one really knows. Even in Florida, where the endangered Florida panther lives in one region and there are almost as many people studying the cats as there are cats, the official count (30 to 50 adults) includes a fudge factor of almost 100 percent.

Until 1993, the cougar was the largest member of the genus *Felis*, but it has since been granted a genus all its own; its scientific name is now *Puma concolor*. Its range is

*The cat's back legs provide the speed and power, while the flexible front legs do the steering and allow the cat to match the split-second maneuvers of deer and other prey.*

*This glorious exemplar of the laws that made the world.*

—ERNEST THOMPSON SETON

stupendous: The cougar lives in the pampas of Patagonia, in the rainforests of Guatemala and in 11 western states, plus Texas, Florida, South Dakota, British Columbia and Alberta. A small number may exist in Saskatchewan.

Occasionally, the cats wander into neighboring states and provinces. Though the official long-distance record is 306 straight-line miles (set by a radio-collared male in Wyoming), a few likely roam much farther. Individuals have reached the Kenai Peninsula in Alaska and—the farthest north—Dawson City in the central Yukon. It is neither the cold nor the shortage of ungulates that prevents cougars from continuing on into the Arctic. The ultimate barrier is the tree line. While the cougar does not absolutely need trees—it survives in the desert, for example, by cleverly using topographic cover to remain invisible—the flat, open tundra neutralizes the element of surprise that is so vital to an ambush hunter. Even within its own range, the cover-loving cat detours around clear-cuts, meadows, pastures and slickrock.

We can learn about cat evolution from DNA samples and about cat diet from scat, but there are only two ways to study the behavior of an animal few people ever see: track it in the snow the old-fashioned way, or fit the cat with a radio-collar. Most studies do both, which is why winter is the usual season for wild-cat fieldwork.

Tracking is the exciting part. "Especially forward tracking," says Jalkotzy, "because you don't know how it's going to turn out." Once, the researcher followed the tracks of a mule deer that had bounded down a snowy slope in great panicked leaps, with a cougar in close pursuit. Then the cougar tracks abruptly disappeared while the deer's mad dash continued. Had the cougar vanished into thin air? "At this point," says Jalkotzy, "the cougar was on the deer's back."

On another occasion, Jalkotzy found three sets of tracks along the same trail: an older set heading outward, a more

*Cougars are excellent swimmers, but they sometimes overestimate their abilities and drown while trying to cross flooded rivers.*

recent set returning and a third fresh set heading out again, this time accompanied by two sets of much smaller tracks. "From this," he explains, "we knew that a female had gone hunting, caught something, then returned, picked up her kittens and led them to the kill site."

When researchers Maurice Hornocker and Wilbur Wiles of Idaho began the first long-term cougar study in 1964, there were no radio-collars available. Instead, they used the old hunting trick of treeing cougars with dogs. Then they tranquilized and ear-tagged the cats. By tracking and treeing them periodically to see which cat was which, they discovered that male cougars were territorial and females

*The biggest cougar on record was an Arizona male that weighed 276 pounds (not counting the intestines) when killed.*

*For a female cougar, parenting is a solitary task with endless responsibilities. For up to two years, she feeds her young, protects them and teaches them the hunting skills they'll need in later life. By the second year, these "kittens" may be bigger and hungrier than she is.*

were less so. More important, they learned that the cats were not disrupting the local deer and elk populations. At that time, this was one of several pioneering wildlife studies which demonstrated that predator and prey lived in balance with one another.

Biologist John Seidensticker joined the Idaho group in 1969 and helped develop the radio-collar that has been so crucial to wild-cat research. Similar devices were already in use in Minnesota and Montana at that time, but since scientists are as protective about new tools as male cougars are about their territories, Seidensticker had to reinvent the collar. For years after, no one could buy a radio-collar without a recommendation. This was partly to foil international smugglers, who were putting tracking devices in drug shipments and kicking them out of airplanes over the American Southwest.

Since then, several in-depth studies have given us our first peek at the world of the cougar. Because actual sightings are rare, the following information has been obtained primarily by plotting radio-collar positions and tracks in the snow: Male territories vary from 25 to 500 square miles, while females claim between 8 and 425 square miles; the best cougar territory may hold one cat per two square miles; a single cat may prowl up to 20 miles a day but more commonly ranges from one to five miles a day. Although these three decades of hard-earned facts haven't given us the personal insights that come from observation, they're a start.

*Following spread: A cougar puts in a rare daytime appearance to scan the bottom of a Utah canyon. Like most cats, a cougar's vision works best at detecting movement. It tells colors apart with difficulty. According to one scientist, it's as if a cougar "cannot believe that anything so negligible as color could be the real cue to where the food is."*

## THE KITTEN AND THE KILLER

The most detailed cougar study ever undertaken has recently shed huge beams of light on one of North America's most secretive mammals. Scientists Ken Logan and Linda Sweanor studied 241 tagged cougars for 10 years in the 1980s and 1990s around the White Sands Missile Range in New Mexico. Of course, the pair didn't have winter snow to help them make step-by-step reconstructions of cougar inter-

actions or kills, but thanks to the open desert, Logan and Sweanor managed to observe the cats more intimately than anyone had before. "Cougars seem to have this high degree of confidence about their hiding skills," Logan reports. "You could tell they didn't think we saw them, even when we were within a few yards." Once, Logan tracked down a female nursing her cubs. As he watched, thrilled, the cubs wrestled with each other and clambered over their mother's head till they fell off in an undignified somersault. Then they took to hunting the twitching tip of Mom's tail with the stalk-and-pounce moves that they would soon be using in earnest on mule deer.

*Cougars hide so well that a paw print in the mud is the only hint of their existence most of us will ever see.*

Before the New Mexico work, cougar "society" was believed to be founded on the principle of mutual avoidance. When a male scraped together a pile of leaves and urinated on it, he was leaving a boundary marker that said unequivocally, "Stay away!" And other males apparently heeded the message. Female zones could overlap each other and those of males, but male-male territories had, at best, common boundaries. Possibly through a time-sharing understanding, different cats visited these mutual boundaries at different times. Territories were considered fairly stable. A cougar's weapons are so formidable that direct conflict was thought to be as unproductive, from an evolutionary point of view, as nuclear war between two superpowers.

It now appears that strife is anything but rare, at least in dense populations. For the New Mexico cats, the greatest source of mortality is territorial conflict. Fierce battles are commonly waged between neighboring males or between a territorial male and an immigrant male looking for a territory. These fights can occur on the boundaries or in the heart of a territory. Males also kill females—sometimes in a battle over prey, sometimes when the female is simply trying to defend her kittens. Occasionally, a male may even

*Twenty pounds of dynamite.*

—STANLEY YOUNG

kill a female as food. Territories shift frequently, and neighbors kill neighbors—usually with a canine bite to the brain. Only the females, which have areas but do not defend "territories" per se, keep the peace with each other.

From playful kitten to deadly serious landowner, the legend is gradually emerging from the shadows.

## THE SURVIVOR: THE BOBCAT

The bobcat is the coyote of the wild-cat world. In a century that has witnessed more extinctions than any time since the Age of Dinosaurs, the bobcat is thriving. Today, *Lynx rufus* goes about its secretive business in southern Canada and in every continental state except Delaware and perhaps Illinois. If it has lost ground in some regions, it has gained in others. It does not need virgin timber; it is small enough to live in any backyard woods. And like all successful animals in modern times, it is quite adaptable. While the bobcat has favorite foods, it eats everything from white-tailed deer and bats to armadillos and golden-crowned kinglets. In one study, bobcats caught more than 40 species of deer, birds and small mammals. It will rarely starve.

Seventeenth-century American colonist Thomas Morton gave us our first description of the bobcat: "a beast like a Catte, but so bigge as a great hound: with a tayle shorter than a Catt. His claws are like a Catts. He will make a pray of the Deare. His flesh is dainty meat, like a lamb. His hide is a choise furre, and accompted a good commodity." The name bobcat comes from its stubby "tayle."

*With intense relish, a desert bobcat gnaws on the leg of a jackrabbit —its favorite meal.*

## FOREVER RIVALS

Distinguishing a bobcat from a lynx might seem, at first glance, to be something like identifying fall warblers: an expert's game. Both are grayish cats with rufous shading on the flanks. Both have short tails and sideboards of facial fur. Both have ear tufts and black-and-white markings on the backs of their ears. The fact that the bobcat's tail is a little longer and its tufts a little shorter is not very helpful.

Fortunately, there are simple ways to tell the cats apart.

**BOBCAT RANGE**

First, consult a map. The lynx is primarily a cat of the deep Canadian and Alaskan woods, but if you see a short-tailed cat in most of the continental United States, it's almost certainly a bobcat. There are 700,000 to 1.5 million bobcats in the Lower 48, but fewer than 700 lynx.

Their ranges overlap primarily in southern Canada, Washington, Idaho, Maine, Minnesota and Colorado. If you spot a cat in one of these regions, look at its feet. A bobcat's feet are proportional to the rest of its body, while its snowbelt cousin has oversized paws. The lynx's hind feet, in particular, look like clown shoes. You may miss the subtle differences between the two species, but you will never miss those feet. They are unmistakable.

As you might expect, bobcats and lynx do not get along. They are too similar. Whenever they meet, the bobcat's scrappy nature usually wins out. That happened during the 1950s when a bridge was built joining Cape Breton Island to mainland Nova Scotia. Until then, Cape Breton had been the preserve of the lynx only, but the bobcat soon displaced the more retiring cat everywhere except in the snowy highlands. Here, the lynx's snowshoe feet gave it the advantage. In an ingenious test, biologist Gerry Parker once attached a spring-loaded gauge to the paws of trapped bobcats and lynx and discovered that the lynx has twice the flotation of its southern rival. Wherever the snow is soft and deep, the lynx will come out on top—literally.

The greatest testimonial to the bobcat's success is that scientists have generally ignored it. Of the three cats, the bobcat is the most common and the least studied. Its one decade of celebrity began in 1975, when an international

*All four legs whirling like windmills, a bobcat somersaults onto its back to use its hind legs to defend itself against a rival lynx. When bobcat and lynx collide, the smaller but more aggressive bobcat usually wins out.*

ban on trade in most spotted cats inflated the price of a bob-cat pelt from less than $50 to almost $600. By the late 1970s, trappers across the United States were taking over 90,000 bobcats annually. Bobcats were suddenly the keystone of a $50-million-a-year industry, and money to study them was not in short supply. Much of what we know about bobcat populations came during those heady days of trapping. When it became clear that there were even more bobcats than had been estimated and that the heavy trapping was not affecting their numbers, the spotlight was switched off, and the doings of our smallest wild cat were once again cloaked in darkness and mystery.

**FACTS AND FANTASIES**

Built like a stocky Celt, the bobcat has short legs and a powerful torso. It averages 15 to 22 pounds. In more gullible times, rumors were rife about slain bobcats that weighed 50 to 70 pounds, but it's unlikely that bobcats have ever exceeded 40 pounds.

Like the cougar, the bobcat has managed to carve a niche in just about every possible habitat. It is equally at home in Texas sage, Georgia canebrakes and Maine oak stands but is most abundant in the Southeast and southern California. It has been estimated that parts of southern Alabama support one bobcat per one-third of a square mile. With that density, you'd think people would be spotting bobcats at every bend in the trail. But they don't. No matter how small the stage, bobcats are magicians at disappearing.

Tom Kitchin and Vicki Hurst, whose photographs appear in this book, once tried to help find a captive bobcat in a small wooded enclosure. I know Tom and Vicki well and have often marveled at how their trained eyes can instantly spot hidden wildlife. When it comes to animals, they,

*A bobcat will watch from a tree, but it rarely, if ever, attacks from above.*

26

# BOBCAT BASICS

| | |
|---|---|
| Scientific name: | *Lynx rufus* |
| Other common names: | bay lynx, wildcat |
| Number of subspecies: | 11 |
| North American population: | 750,000-1.5 million |
| Length with tail: | 30-36 inches |
| Weight: | males, 19-22 pounds; females, 14-15 pounds |
| Habitat: | forests of southern Canada through the American Southwest, coastal rainforest, sagebrush steppe, swampland |
| Size of territory: | 1-42 square miles |
| Diet: | often rabbits and hares, but known to eat more than 40 kinds of prey, including deer, birds, reptiles and small mammals, such as squirrels, mice, voles and bats |
| Gestation: | 62 days |
| Size of litter: | 2-3; maximum 5 |
| Birth weight of young: | 10-12 ounces |
| Time with mother: | 9 months |
| Life span: | 12-15 years in the wild |

too, are magicians—of observation. Yet both of them, together with the bobcat's owner, spent three hours scouring the 100-by-60-yard lot and could not find the missing cat.

Home ranges of all cats, including bobcats, partly depend on how much prey an area supports. In southern California, where the food is abundant, these ranges may be less than one square mile. In the slim pickings of the northern woods, one bobcat may need 40 square miles. Much as it clashes with our romantic view of wild cats as big-country roamers, most bobcats would probably be happy with a territory no bigger than a large barnyard, as long as the chickens and calves were constantly replenished.

A male's territory is two to five times larger than that of the female. Both male and female ranges may increase dramatically if a bobcat "inherits" a neighboring range after the death of its owner. Female bobcat ranges usually do not overlap. It's not clear whether the bobcat's tempestuous personality is behind this cool approach to sisterhood, but female bobcats do brawl on occasion. Two Colorado biologists observed one radio-collared female grappling with an unknown female for almost half an hour. As in most domestic cat fights, short, intense bouts of flying fur

*Following spread: A denizen of semi-open habitat, the bobcat has lived in every continental state except Delaware. It is a relatively recent immigrant to Canada.*

*"The kittenlike wonder of those big, mild eyes."*

—Ernest Thompson Seton

alternated with long, almost studious sizing-up periods.

The bobcat's reputation as a scrapper is the stuff of legend. Anyone who can "lick his weight in wild cats" is formidable indeed. Natural historians, from John James Audubon onward, have emphasized the bobcat's "perpetual ill humor" and described the cat as a "spitfire demon with a perennial growl and a physiognomy distorted with diabolic rage when approached." In all likelihood, they were referring to a bobcat in a trap—certainly not a situation in which an animal could be expected to show its gentler side. (Incredible as it may sound, one Texan who climbed a tree to, as he put it, "punch out" a bobcat later expressed surprise at its viciousness when it attacked him.)

An unnatural but perhaps better gauge of a bobcat's true character comes from the reports of the many people who have raised bobcats as pets. "They're just like house cats, only harder on the sofa," quips one biologist. In his 1958 book, *The Bobcat of North America*, Stanley Young was slightly more reserved, but one detects a certain affection beneath his gruff appraisal: "To tame a bobcat requires the patience of a Job and the gentleness of a St. Francis—and a little insurance on the fingers might be in order."

## THE INTROVERT: THE LYNX

The northern woods have always drawn their share of hermits, but none shyer than the lynx. As with the bearded recluses who used to hide out from their mysterious pasts in Alaska and the Yukon, no one is quite sure of the lynx's origin. Like those recluses, the lynx goes about its business, troubling no one. And when changing times rob it of its solitude, it answers by retreating deeper into the woods.

*Lynx canadensis* lives mainly in the dark, unbroken forests of Canada and Alaska. Although it is just half the size of the typically 45-pound European lynx, the two are close cousins. Size is one of the few species' qualities that sometimes seem to change almost overnight. Once it settled in our northern woods and began feeding mainly on

*Eyes fixed on some potential prey, a lynx gazes out from the gloom of the northern woods. While the cougar has the intense face of a predator and the bobcat a confident competitor's gaze, a lynx typically looks shy, almost gentle.*

hare rather than deer, the original lynx probably scaled itself down within a few thousand years.

The lynx has the proportions of a basketball player—big jackrabbit hind legs (an example of the predator imitating its prey), gangly frame and size-18 paws. Wide muttonchops of fur make its face more impressive in any confrontation. In some older animals, this wheel of facial fur ends in a white forked goatee that imparts a look of thoughtfulness. Of our three wild cats, the lynx varies the least in color from place to place. In Alaska or in Maine, the lynx is a smoky gray, with black-tipped ears and tail and russet edgings along the flanks.

A day in the life of a lynx begins just before dawn, which is the lynx's most active time. As it rambles through the snowy woods, it usually walks along the length of every log it comes upon. Its huge, furry knuckles look almost arthritic as it spreads them. With these magnificent paws, the lynx floats on snow that has wolves and foxes floundering up to their chests. Its feet are almost as big as a wolf's,

*The essence of cathood: A male lynx hugs the shadows. North America's wild cats rarely linger in the open and will make wide detours to avoid cutting across meadows and pastures. Little wonder that all we ever see of them are glimpses.*

# LYNX BASICS

| | |
|---|---|
| Scientific name: | *Lynx canadensis* |
| Number of subspecies: | 2 |
| North American population: | 300-700 in Lower 48; Canada and Alaska unknown |
| Length with tail: | 30-40 inches |
| Weight: | males, 25-35 pounds; females, 15-20 pounds |
| Habitat: | northern woods in United States and boreal forest in Canada |
| Size of territory : | 2.5-92 square miles; usually 7-35 square miles |
| Diet: | mainly snowshoe hare; also deer, grouse, squirrel |
| Gestation: | 70 days |
| Size of litter: | 1-5; usually 4; maximum 8 |
| Birth weight of young: | 12-13 ounces |
| Time with mother: | 9 months |
| Life span: | up to 15 years in the wild, but usually 10 years or less |

yet this fine-boned cat weighs only one-quarter as much.

When the lynx comes to a birch stand, a willow edge or any other promising "rabbitat," it pokes around with the care of a bookkeeper checking ledger entries. If a hare flushes, the lynx tears after it in 6-to-10-foot bounds, propelled by powerful rear legs that dangle down, harelike, at the height of each leap. The drama of life or death ends quickly, one way or the other. After about five leaps, the lynx either gives up or has knocked the hare off balance with one swipe of its big paw. Then it lunges forward to deliver a quick killing bite to the back of the neck. Members of the dog family often eat their prey to death, but like all cats, the lynx executes first and dines afterward.

A lynx must chase between 3 and 10 hares before catching one, so it is not unusual when the first pursuit fails. Every so often, other forces come between the cat and its prey. A great horned owl may station itself nearby, ready to scoop up a hare that the lynx routs. Some winters ago, caribou biologist Alasdair Veitch was part of a helicopter survey in Labrador when the low-flying craft passed over a lynx in full pursuit of a hare. "They both stopped in their tracks," reports Veitch, "and the lynx looked up at us with what can only be described as disgust while the hare ran off through the trees, no doubt thinking that God is a large red-and-white bird that makes a terrible noise."

Shortly after daybreak, the lynx begins to indulge seri-

_LYNX RANGE_

ously in that most catlike of pastimes—sleeping. It may conceal itself near a hare trail just in case, a good strategy in abundant-hare years. On summer days, it retreats to the shade of the cool forest. In winter, although its thick fur affords ample warmth, it may seek out a sunny slope to take the edge off the chill air.

Near sunset, the lynx stirs again. A healthy adult usually catches something—a hare, a grouse, a red squirrel, even a fox if the snow is deep—every day or two. It is intensely curious about little things fluttering in the wind, a weakness that trappers have long exploited. A bit of ribbon or tin foil on a bush is sure to catch the sharp eye of any lynx in the vicinity. In the four centuries of the fur trade, curiosity has killed many a cat.

The lynx's day continues after dark, although it is not as active at night as it is at the corners of the day. In its wanderings, it rarely strays more than 100 yards from trees. Some researchers think that its reticent personality comes from the lack of intense competition from the bears, cougars and other aggressive predators that forged the bobcat's fiery temperament. But wolves do share those same northern woods, and so the lynx is never at ease without an escape tree within bounding distance.

Ernest Thompson Seton wrote of one lynx that strayed a little too far from the safety of the woods. The famous naturalist wanted a picture of it, so one of his companions, a good runner, actually outsprinted the lynx over 200 yards and drove it back toward Seton. The lynx was lucky: The cost of its mistake was merely having to pose uncomfortably for a few snapshots. Wolves—open-country run-

*In the final stage of a hunt, a lynx's patient stalking gives way to instant acceleration. If it doesn't catch its prey after five or six bounds, it usually gives up the chase.*

ners par excellence—would have exacted a different price.

The lynx may shun open areas, but several observers have commented on its uncatlike readiness to take to water. Lynx tracks have been spotted leading into the frigid Yukon River and out again on the opposite bank, almost two miles across. An isolated case of a lynx on Baffin Island suggests that it may occasionally swim even farther. Reportedly, the lynx swims "faster than a dog but slower than a caribou."

With its meticulous hunting style, the lynx covers about 1½ to 3 miles a day. But when food is scarce in its local area, a lynx just keeps going…and going. One lynx from Great Slave Lake in the Northwest Territories turned up near

35

*With a snowshoe hare firmly gripped in its jaws, a lynx trots off to enjoy the day's meal. To avoid tripping, the lynx adjusts its gait to the swinging of the hare and widens the stance of its front paws as if it were bowlegged.*

*At left, a lynx investigates its reflection in a pond. A tentative smack of the paw is one way a cat sizes up an unfamiliar object.*

Edmonton, Alberta, almost 700 miles to the south. This built-in readiness to roam is vital to the survival of the lynx, because its chief prey, the snowshoe hare, prefers forests 5 to 50 years after a fire—and who knows where the latest fire has been? In some decades, government policies of suppressing all forest fires have hurt both the lynx and the hare populations.

There are only two reported lynx attacks on people, but they both sound like cases of mistaken identity—on the part of the lynx. One November afternoon in 1974, Newfoundland trapper Boyd Duffett was tramping home through the woods with 12 snowshoe hares over his left shoulder when a female lynx sprang onto his back from a balsam fir tree. Duffett battled the cat for 10 minutes before managing to strangle it. He escaped with just a few scratches.

The second case is similar: During a snowstorm in the early 1900s, a lynx attacked a man wearing buckskin clothing, apparently mistaking him for a deer.

# CHAPTER

## 2

# BONES OF CONTENTION

"IF A COUGAR AND A JAGUAR WALKED INTO A ROOM, YOU'D have no trouble telling them apart," says Kevin Seymour, a vertebrate paleontologist at the Royal Ontario Museum in Toronto, Ontario. "But just try to distinguish them from their bones." Seymour is attempting to explain why the cat's family tree is such a mess.

To paleontologists, all cats look pretty much alike. To make matters worse, cats are thought to have evolved in tropical forests, where fossils rarely form. As a result, whole lineages may rest on the analysis of the lower jawbone, the most frequently found wild-cat remnant. Finally, all modern felines evolved rapidly within the past 12 million years, and in evolutionary terms, that's a blink of an eye.

Why should it be more difficult to tell two wild cats apart than, for example, a wolf and a coyote? It's because felines are far more specialized than other meat-eaters. Most carnivores are, to varying degrees, omnivorous, and their body structure reflects this evolutionary hedging of bets. But in cats, it's as if nature found the formula for the perfect killer. A short muzzle allows the cat to exert a more powerful bite than a long muzzle, so all cats have a short face. All have powerful rear springs for pouncing and front hooks for hanging on while their specialized teeth deliver the *coup de grâce*. This design was so successful that through all the cat's many experimental forms, the original leap-and-pierce formula was retained. A house cat, a cougar and the first cat on

*The body of the cat evolved for one purpose—hunting. It is so specialized that the world's 37 cat species differ very little from one another.*

Earth have much in common. They differ mainly in size.

The earliest-known cat lived about 34 million years ago. Named *Proailurus*, it was the size of a small bobcat. In the past 12 million years, all the modern species we know today, as well as many more, evolved. Giant cats roamed from the southern tip of Baja California to the northern slope of Alaska. The biggest ones, the huge American lions and the famous saber-toothed cats, went extinct around 10,000 years ago, along with their Ice Age prey. Smaller cats such as the cougar—which, like the leopard in Africa today, had till then been a "B" team predator—suddenly vaulted to the top of the food chain.

Until recently, many scientists separated all modern cat species into two convenient genuses: the Big Cats and the Small Cats. Big Cats roared and had round pupils; Small Cats purred and had slit pupils. The cougar, lynx and bobcat were all Small Cats, although the cougar had round pupils and was bigger than some Big Cats. It doesn't sound very precise, and it wasn't. Adding to the confusion were

*Cats such as the lynx originated in forests where fossils rarely form, so the feline family tree has always been somewhat murky. Recent genetic work is helping clear up some of the mysteries.*

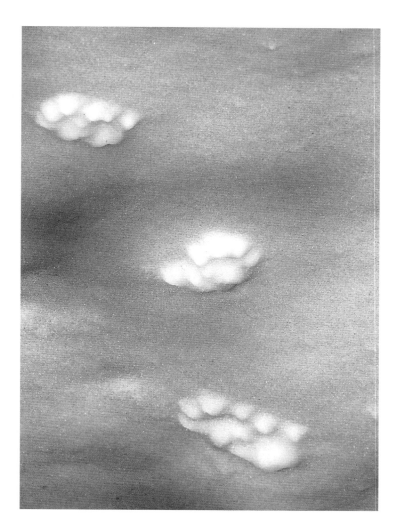

*The lynx's huge paws evolved in recent times. Thanks to these natural snowshoes, the lynx can hunt the deep powder zones that bobcats, coyotes and foxes avoid.*

a half-dozen other proposed systems, which divided the cats into anywhere from 3 to 20 genuses.

**THE TWO "C'S"**  Which cat evolved where continues to be a matter of debate, but a new measuring tool has appeared. The National Cancer Institute in Frederick, Maryland, is an unlikely world leader in wild-cat discoveries. Until the 1970s, the facility was an army base that specialized in research on biological warfare. The buildings are still barrackslike, but the work done there today is very different. In the Laboratory of Genomic Diversity, under the direction of Dr. Stephen O'Brien, about 85 researchers explore possible

*What astonished him was that cats should have two holes cut in their coats exactly at the places where their eyes were.*

—G.C. LICHTENBERG, *REFLECTIONS*

*A cougar may live up to 20 years in captivity, but in the wild, the known record is 12 years 8 months. In heavily hunted areas, even a 7-year-old cougar is rare.*

genetic solutions to cancer. Another 15 are working on the family tree of cats.

What do cancer and cats have in common? Mapping the DNA sequences of various species lays the groundwork for gene therapy, one of the most promising fields of medicine for the 21st century. Twenty years ago, while investigating feline leukemia, O'Brien became fascinated by cats. From domestic subjects, he soon turned his attention to the DNA of wild felines. According to O'Brien, wild cats are exposed to the same diseases as are humans but have developed a resistance to them through genetic solutions.

Species DNA accumulates mutations over time. The rate of mutation, says O'Brien, is like a "molecular clock" that can tell us roughly when one species diverged from another. Thanks to welcome funding from nontraditional donors to cancer research, such as the World Wildlife Fund, O'Brien and his colleagues have been able to pursue groundbreaking research into both "C's."

This research has revealed that the closest living relative of the cheetah is the cougar. (Before this, the oddly built cheetah was thought to have branched off early from the main line of cats.) Lynx and bobcats, meanwhile, are closely related to lions and tigers. In the next few years, thanks to DNA sequencing and O'Brien's extracurricular interests, the feline family tree may look a lot less tangled.

DNA can last a long time. It has been extracted from old museum cougar skins, from Egyptian mummies, even from 14,000-year-old saber-toothed cats unearthed in the Rancho La Brea tarpits in Los Angeles. But in more ancient fossils, minerals have replaced the organic matter, so unfortunately, we're back to comparing tiny differences in lower jawbones.

**THE CHICKEN OR THE EGG?**

It is usually thought that cats, like people, migrated over the Bering land bridge into North America, then spread into South America. Some certainly did, but over time, there must

### HOW FAR CAN THEY JUMP?

| | |
|---|---|
| Human, world-record long jump: | 29.36 feet |
| Cougar: | 30 feet |
| Bobcat: | 12 feet |
| Lynx: | 15 feet |

### HOW HIGH CAN THEY JUMP?

| | |
|---|---|
| Human, world-record high jump: | 8.04 feet |
| Cougar: | 18 feet |
| Bobcat: | 8 feet |
| Lynx: | 8 feet |

### HOW FAST CAN THEY RUN?

| | |
|---|---|
| Human, world-record 100 meters: | 9.84 seconds |
| Cougar, 100 meters: | 4.7 seconds (45 mph) |
| Bobcat, 100 meters: | 7.46 seconds (30 mph) |
| Lynx, 100 meters: | 7.46 seconds (30 mph) |

have been reverse traffic as well. With many cats, this has created a chicken-or-the-egg puzzle: Did the primordial cheetah cross into North America and evolve into the cougar, or did some primeval North American cougar travel into Eurasia and give rise to the cheetah? Even within the western hemisphere, the cougar could have spread from North America south or from South America north. All we know for sure is that from three to one million years ago, a longer-legged cougar roamed North America. Our modern cougar first appeared about 300,000 years ago.

Both bobcat and lynx are close cousins of the European cat (*Lynx lynx*). Some researchers—the two-genus crowd—go so far as to call all three cats variants of the same species. The bobcat has been in North America for at least 600,000 years, while the lynx arrived less than 200,000 years ago. Beyond this, their appearance on the North American scene is shrouded in mystery. The lynx, the shyest of the three, was also shy when it came to leaving fossils. As for the bobcat, its origins are so murky that one paleontologist groaned in mock anguish when I merely mentioned the bobcat's name, as you or I might groan if a lovable troublemaker we know walked into the room.

Blaire Van Valkenburgh, one of the world's experts in carnivore evolution, describes the frustrating process of analyzing the first record of the lynx clan in North America. This important 2½-million-year-old fossil may be the direct relative of the bobcat: "You have this little jaw, and you figure, well, it's about the size of a bobcat. It could be a bobcat. Of course, it could also be an ocelot." Although it was a toss-up, in the end, the scientists decided to call it a bobcat—for now—which is why some books state that the bobcat has been in North America for 2½ million years.

Those elusive cats. No wonder my paleontologist friend groaned.

## THE PHYSICAL CAT

EARS. A cat hears higher frequencies than humans do, thanks to superior design. It also hears fainter sounds, because its big external ears, or pinnae, amplify in the same way that cupping our hands to our ears does. Thirty muscles (compared to our six) swivel the ears quickly to pinpoint any noise.

EAR TUFTS. Sensitive to vibration, tufts act like antennas to help lynx and bobcats localize more precisely the sounds made by small prey.

WHISKERS. A cat can't focus well at close range in the dark, but its whiskers (24 on average) help feel the way by touch and by air currents. Unlike other carnivores, the cat never evolved whiskers under its chin because it rarely lowers its head to pick up a scent.

EYES. A cat's night vision is six times better than ours, and its bulging corneas also give it better peripheral vision. Like most nocturnal hunters, however, a cat's sense of color is poor.

SKIN. Thick and loose, a cat's skin affords protection during a fight.

SPINE. Vertebrae are held together largely by muscles rather than ligaments, as ours are, so a cat's backbone is extremely flexible and can lengthen, contract, arch, even twist.

HEART. A relatively small heart makes the cat a sprinter, not a long-distance runner. After a chase, it may need 20 minutes to catch its breath.

TEETH. Of the typical cat's 28 teeth, eight are crucial: the four long canines are for puncturing

*Above: The cougar's luxuriant tail improves balance, and in females with young, it also serves unofficially as the kittens' favorite toy. Far left: A cougar displays its formidable weaponry. Top left: Although the bobcat was named for its bobbed tail, its tail is actually longer than the lynx's, bottom left.*

and gripping, and the four carnassials at the rear snip the meat into pieces like two pairs of garden shears. When a cat chews with its head to one side, it is using its carnassials.

GUMS. When a cat snarls, the black gum line makes its impressive teeth look even more dangerous.

HIND LEGS. These powerful springs give the cat a faster start than its hoofed prey.

FRONT LEGS. A cat walks or runs by moving the front and rear legs on one side forward at the same time, then advancing the front and rear legs on the other side.

HEEL. The cat walks on its toes, unlike humans and bears, which walk flat-footed. What looks like a backward-pointing knee is actually its heel.

CLAWS. A pulley system of tendons allows the cat to walk with its claws retracted to keep them sharp. But like folded switchblades, the claws can spring into action at a moment's notice.

COLLARBONE. Vestigial. The forelimbs are attached directly to the shoulder blades, which gives superior flexibility, allowing the cat to turn on a dime to keep up with a prey's evasive maneuvers and also permitting its characteristic belly-to-the-ground stalk.

TAIL. The cougar uses its tail the way some people use their hands—to express itself. The tail also serves as a balancing pole. Although the bobcat was named after its "bobbed," or sawed-off, tail, the lynx's tail is even shorter, probably because of its cold-weather habitat.

# CHAPTER 3

# ON THE PROWL

THE HOLY GRAIL OF EVERY SAFARI-GOER IN AFRICA IS TO see a lion make a kill in the wild. The odds of success are slim, but every year, a few tourists get their wish. While researching this book, my Holy Grail was far more modest: to find someone who had witnessed a kill by a wild cougar, bobcat or lynx. After all, if cats are the ultimate predators, the kill must be the climax of their days.

In my quest, I spoke to about a hundred biologists, trappers and wilderness guides. I placed requests for information in outdoor magazines and posted ads in wildlife corners of the Internet. No luck. No one reported having seen this event, although I was told that researchers have observed cougars killing guanacos —a relative of the llama—on the open pampas of southern Argentina.

As it turns out, virtually everything we know about cats on the prowl has been inferred from tracks in the snow, from studying radio-collared cats at a kill site after the deed is done and from the unappetizing analysis of a dead cat's stomach and scat samples. A wild cat catching prey seems to operate by the same mysterious physics as a spinning electron: If you're in a position to see it, you never will.

Luckily, my quest for the Grail was not entirely in vain. The cats have raised their veil of secrecy on a number of occasions.

*Although speed and agility are crucial in the final chase, North American cats rely on the element of surprise as their prime weapon. Even a pintail duck, seemingly protected by wings and water, was no match for this bobcat's sudden strike.*

*Cat claws retract into protective scabbards, which keeps them from becoming blunt. A unique mechanical system of ligaments and tendons allows a cat to curl its toes without extending its claws. Retractable claws also permit silent stalking, since only the soft pads touch the ground.*

## FEAST OR FAMINE

Like most carnivores, the three forest cats live by a feast-or-famine regime. Wise investors of effort, cats can hunt for weeks on little food. And when they make a kill, they are chow hounds. A cougar routinely packs away 18 pounds of meat at a sitting. Over a long winter, a cougar may *average* as much as 13 pounds a day. Even a 20-pound lynx consumes at least 1½ pounds daily. Such a hefty intake reflects the cat's high-energy needs as well as its rapid digestive system, which processes the meal too quickly to extract every calorie and nutrient.

The cat's ability to gorge has practical advantages. Dead prey sends an unmistakable olfactory signal to the entire forest community: Meal here! Cougars, bobcats and lynx (unlike leopards) generally do not haul their meal up into the relative safety of a tree. It is therefore to their benefit to pack away as much as possible before the sharp noses of wolves or bears home in. Even the cougar usually retreats before such dangerous opposition.

As a bonus, fast feeding also minimizes the effects of weather on dead prey. Cold presents a particular problem for wild cats. One bitter Idaho winter, biologist John Seidensticker witnessed a cougar sleeping on top of an elk carcass, presumably to keep it unfrozen for the next round of feeding.

## A DANGEROUS PROFESSION

Cats are generally thought of as partly ambush hunters that lie in wait and partly stalkers that creep and pounce, but their travel style suggests they are also flushers. Cats often seem to meander unpredictably throughout their territory. Noting this, an early paper referred to the bobcat as an "aimless hunter." Aimless? Who knows how many grouse and rabbits it bumps into and catches during these wanderings?

The lynx is an even greater practitioner of the art of random discovery. A female lynx and her older kittens may sometimes fan out like a search team. If one acciden-

*Ambush hunters such as the cougar don't target the sick or weak, as do many predators; they target the unwary.*

tally flushes a hare, it gives chase—and if the unfortunate hare outstrips the original pursuer, it often bounds into the waiting claws of another.

It is easy to imagine that in this game of life and death, the predator holds all the cards—and the worst that can happen is a missed meal. But wasted effort is the least of a big cat's worries. It may sometimes pay for a botched attempt with its life. In one incident, both predator and prey tumbled off a cliff during a wild struggle. Another time, a cougar was fatally impaled in the neck by a branch. On a third occasion, a panic-stricken deer fled headlong past a tree with a cougar clinging to its side. The cougar

crashed into the tree and broke its back. The deer escaped.

Because of the size of their prey, cougars are particularly vulnerable. Deer and elk are high-risk meals—one wrong move, and the entrée may spike the cougar mortally in the lung or abdomen. Even a broken bone can prove fatal, because a limping cat is no longer able to hunt effectively. As a result, a predator never attacks without first evaluating the risks. On some level, it knows that it must avoid injury.

*Just as we cover leftovers with plastic wrap, a cougar will bury a deer carcass in leaves and twigs between feedings. For the cougar, however, it's a gesture of possession rather than an attempt to preserve the flavor.*

## THE PREDATOR-IN-CHIEF

The cougar has been called the best hunter in the world. It probably is. A solitary 100-pound female can take down an 800-pound elk. No other big predator can fell seven or eight times its own weight. As for hunting success, researcher Maurice Hornocker observed that on the final stalk, Idaho cougars bring down a deer or an elk 8 out of 10 times. By contrast, African lions have an overall success rate of only 1 out of 10 times.

How did the cougar get to be so good? It has a lot to

*A cougar is like a light breeze in the country. At first, you're not aware it's there. But as you slowly become more attuned, you begin to feel it on the back of your neck.*

—John Seidensticker

do with the challenging environment of the New World. African cats can afford to be sloppy hunters, because if they miss one wildebeest, there are 600,000 more on the same savanna. North American forests typically are much less fertile, and the cougar has evolved superior stealth to make every strike count. Infinitely patient, a cougar may spend half a day quietly watching, almost dead-still. Only the black tip of its tail twitches involuntarily with excitement. It prefers to wait until its prey is within 30 feet before committing itself. It fares poorly if the chase begins from more than 60 feet away.

Some biologists have speculated about the wild cat's ability to kill instantly by driving apart two vertebrae with a well-placed bite. Supposedly, its nerve-rich canine teeth guide its jaws like radar to the vital spot on the victim's neck. John Seidensticker has doubts about this smart-bite theory. He notes that some foreign big cats just crunch the vertebrae rather than pry them apart with elegant precision. The surgical neck bite may figure with small game, but the cougar usually dispatches large prey by clamping shut the windpipe from the front of the neck. Occasionally, an elk dies when its head hits the ground during the cougar's high-impact strike.

Diet varies by season and by region. Cougars eat mule deer in the west and wild hogs and white-tailed deer in Florida. In Idaho, they hunt mainly mule deer and elk in winter and Columbian ground squirrels in summer. Because female elk tend to herd in the open, cougars often target the lone but more powerful bulls. As a rule of thumb, a cougar takes a deer, a sheep or an elk every 7 to 10 days. In between, it snacks on porcupines, hares and other bite-sized prey. In one California study, that added up to 48 deer and 58 smaller animals a year. Some mountain lions are better hunters than others and specialize in deer, while others eke out an existence on smaller prey.

One major kill every week and a half is a pretty laid-

*A biology professor once placed a box of bones on the table in front of him, reports nature writer George Laycock. The box was 17 inches long, 12 inches wide and 4 inches deep, about the size of an average compact disk player. "This is the complete skeleton —skull and all—of an adult mountain lion," explained the professor. "That's all there is. The animal is all muscle and sinew."*

back regimen, often involving fewer than three straight-line miles of travel a day. (One biologist described the cougar's mellow attitude: "Why walk when you can lie down?") Females with yearlings are under far more pressure. They must kill a deer every two to three days.

When it makes a big kill, the cougar stays nearby for several days. One young Idaho female was so pleased with her cow elk that she didn't leave its side for three weeks. Usually, though, the cats bed down a few hundred yards from the kill, covering it with leaves or duff in their absence. The instinct to cover is strong. In an almost pathetic gesture, a female in some barren Arizona tract placed one lonely twig on a deer carcass before heading off.

The mere presence of a cougar in the neighborhood doesn't seem to disturb deer or elk, but the effect of a kill is striking. Potential prey leave the area immediately. To compensate, the cougar moves to the farthest reaches of its territory for the next round of hunting.

## MISUNDER-STANDINGS

Nowadays, we take "the balance of nature" for granted, and we expect cougars (and bobcats and lynx) to live in equilibrium with their chief prey. In fact, they do. But not long ago, predators were thought to operate like deadly epidemics, annihilating their victims, then moving on. This misunderstanding led to the disaster on the Kaibab Plateau in Arizona, which has become almost as famous an environmental event as the disappearance of the dodo.

When the Kaibab became a natural game reserve in 1906, the first order of business was to eliminate all predators. After 25 years, 781 cougars and almost every other meat-eater that walked or flew had been destroyed. Without any natural checks, the original healthy population of 4,000 mule deer turned into a blight of 100,000 hoofed locusts that devoured almost every leaf, twig, flower and blade of grass. Mass starvation followed, and by 1940, only 10,000 mule deer remained. Like the extinction of the dodo, sim-

*Sizing up a potentially dangerous snack, a cougar tries to out-maneuver a treed porcupine. Sometimes, it manages to slip a paw beneath the porcupine and rake open its unprotected belly. Other times, it just comes away with a painful pawful of quills.*

ilar miscalculations have occurred not once but many times.

Ranchers have always been sworn enemies of cougars, because the big cats sometimes prey on hoofstock. There are even accounts of occasional killing sprees—a mountain lion in Nevada once slaughtered 59 sheep in one night. In the cat's natural world, such behavior exists to take advantage of rare good luck—for example, when another deer blunders past shortly after a first is killed. It becomes a problem only in the artificial situation of a high density of domestic animals unable to escape. In this case, the innocent misunderstanding is the cougar's.

## THE LYNX AND THE HARE: A CLASSIC CYCLE REVISITED

You can't write about lynx without the snowshoe hare poking its twitching nose into the story. For a hundred years, the lynx-hare cycle has stood as the textbook example of a predator-prey relationship: First, the hares multiply. The lynx eat the hares. As a benefit of a plentiful food source, the lynx multiply. The hare population crashes. The lynx population crashes. The hares begin to multiply. And the cycle goes on and on.

That's the standard version in a nutshell, but let's dig a little deeper into this remarkable story. It isn't always so neat and predictable.

Where it occurs, the cycle averages 9.6 years. Astonishingly, the cycle is synchronous across North America. In other words, the cycle usually peaks in Alaska and in Ontario in the same year. Although there is sometimes a one-to-two-year lag between regions, the timing is never unrelated. By contrast, that other famous boom-and-bust creature of the North, the lemming, peaks in different years in different areas.

High and low densities vary over time and from place to place. One peak in the Northwest Territories produced 2,000 hares and one lynx per square mile. Meanwhile, a similar peak in Alberta recorded a population of only one lynx every four square miles. In some decades,

*A cat's sandpapery tongue is mainly a body-cleaning tool, but it's also useful when eating. The rough spikelets on the upper surface, called papillae, rasp meat from the bones.*

such as the 1970s, the population spikes are huge; you're practically tripping over snowshoe hares, and lynx are as common as foxes. In other decades, the peaks are so small that they're barely noticeable.

The dramatic cycle begins with the hare. When times are good, hares are reproductive machines, producing two or three litters a year, often with 12 leverets in each litter. When their numbers peak (at about eight hares per football field of good habitat), the hares have stripped almost every bud and new twig. Now, the willows and alders they feed on begin to generate bitter compounds that inhibit digestion. The plants, in short, begin to fight back. Many

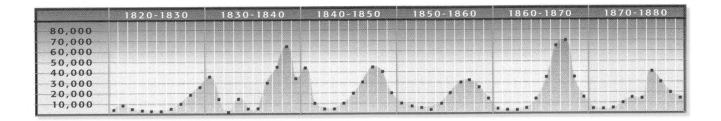

| 1820-1830 | 1830-1840 | 1840-1850 | 1850-1860 | 1860-1870 | 1870-1880 |

80,000
70,000
60,000
50,000
40,000
30,000
20,000
10,000

## THE LYNX CYCLE 1820-1994

No one knows how many lynx live in the northern woods, but for almost two centuries, Canadian fur traders have recorded the number of lynx trapped annually.* These figures clearly show that the lynx population follows a 10-year boom-and-bust cycle. They also reveal the human impact on the cycle.

* The gap between 1908 and 1918 coincides with the switchover from Hudson's Bay Company records to government records.

hares starve or fall prey to burgeoning lynx populations, as well as owls, wolves and foxes. At the same time, hare reproduction plummets. A year or two later, a massive lynx die-off follows across the now unrabbited North.

Exactly what happens to the lynx has been the subject of intense research over the past 25 years. It was once thought that most of the lynx simply starved to death. Old natural-history books rang with accounts of gaunt, hollow-eyed lynx staggering about in the snow. Although this may occur, there are more important forces at work. Young female lynx no longer reproduce, and the litters

*While the lynx normally hunts alone, it is the only North American cat known to cooperate with others of its kind. Usually, these hunting parties consist of a mother and her older kittens, but sometimes, a male and a female or even two family groups travel and hunt together.*

58

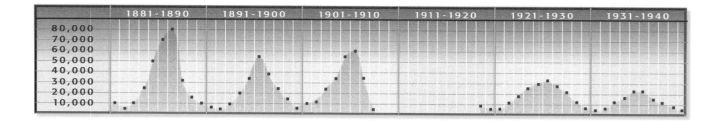

| | 1881-1890 | 1891-1900 | 1901-1910 | 1911-1920 | 1921-1930 | 1931-1940 |
|---|---|---|---|---|---|---|
| 80,000 | | | | | | |
| 70,000 | | | | | | |
| 60,000 | | | | | | |
| 50,000 | | | | | | |
| 40,000 | | | | | | |
| 30,000 | | | | | | |
| 20,000 | | | | | | |
| 10,000 | | | | | | |

In the simpler era of the 19th century, the cycle was at its most natural, with high, sharp peaks and low valleys. By 1930, the difference between the up years and the down years had diminished significantly. These low numbers are thought to be a result of overtrapping during the low part of the cycle. Once the core population is decimated at its most vulnerable time, the effect may persist for decades.

*Snowshoe hares make up anywhere from 40 to 85 percent of a lynx's diet. On average, a lynx kills two hares every three days.*

of older females do not survive. Lynx also move more. During a hare crash, a core population of lynx may stay put, but many others expand their home ranges or give them up altogether and try to survive as nomads. They also begin to take greater risks: Most of the lynx sightings in northern towns are made during hare lows.

**SNAPPING THE CYCLE**

Not all lynx follow this 10-year cycle. One study in Newfoundland discovered that lynx switched to a mainly caribou diet when the local hare population crashed, then switched back when the hares returned. However,

| 1941-1950 | 1951-1960 | 1961-1970 | 1971-1980 | 1981-1990 | 1991-1994 |

80,000
70,000
60,000
50,000
40,000
30,000
20,000
10,000

# THE LYNX CYCLE

After 1930, the cycle was almost invisible for 25 years, but by the 1960s, the population seemed to have recovered, possibly because of stricter trapping quotas. The flat line since the mid-1980s reflects low fur prices, not low lynx numbers. The lynx cycle peaks at roughly the same time across the whole country but lags behind the snowshoe hare cycle by a year or two. For example, 1903 was a peak year for the snowshoe hare; the corresponding lynx peak came in 1905.

the Newfoundland situation is exceptional, and over most of its range, the lynx hunts deer only occasionally. In a very informal estimate, biologist Kim Poole says that of 1,000 prey captures, lynx may take 850 hares, 149 squirrels, grouse and ptarmigan and 1 ungulate. In Alaska, that ungulate is a caribou or Dall's sheep; in eastern Canada, a caribou or white-tailed deer; in the west, a mule deer.

Although no one has witnessed such a kill, evidence in the snow has allowed biologists to reconstruct some of these epic life-and-death struggles. The lynx sometimes "rides" the animal's back for a quarter of a mile until it succeeds in biting an artery or the deer or caribou perishes from an accumulation of wounds. "Some caribou looked as if they had 200 little pinpricks in them," recalls Alaskan biologist Bob Stephenson. "It must have been like having a cat on your face, flailing away."

In some parts of the continent, the hare-lynx cycle simply never occurs. In the Lower 48, for example, snowshoe hare habitat is limited, so hares never explode to 20 to 40 times their number as they do in the great northland. The typical tenfold increase of lynx likewise never happens here. Instead, both live at low densities. There are no peaks, only valleys. While this may be due to fragmented habitat, it is not necessarily an unnatural condition. Animals on the fringe of their ranges often live differently than those in the core. Some researchers also believe that the peaks are a recent evolutionary "bonus," that the low-density years are the cat's original state. This makes the lynx not the victim of the hare cycle but the profiteer.

## THE CYCLING BOBCAT?

The bobcat's diet matches its game-for-anything personality. Some years, some places, it is a master of the smorgasbord. But it can also adhere to the same one-note diet as a lynx. Sometimes, it even cycles like a lynx.

In Idaho, for example, the bobcat favors blacktailed jackrabbits, which follow the same 10-year ups and downs as the snowshoe hare. When the jackrabbits are flush, the bobcats boom. When the jackrabbits disappear, so do the bobcats. During hard times, bobcats go on the same long marches as lynx. "The only difference," says biologist Steve Knick, "is that during peaks, bobcats can't crank out the young at the same pace that lynx can." In this part of North America, however, the remnant lynx and their snowshoe hare partners do *not* cycle to the same extent.

In the Northeast, the bobcat dines mainly on snowshoe hares, with a little deer on the side. The attacks on deer usually occur in winter, when a stalking cat is at its most silent and the deer are weak and hindered by snow. A bobcat can also catch a deer in its bed. Newborn fawns, in

*Possessively, almost affectionately, a tired bobcat curls up for a snooze with a captured ruffed grouse. After all the effort of hunting, the bobcat is determined to safeguard its prize from scavengers.*

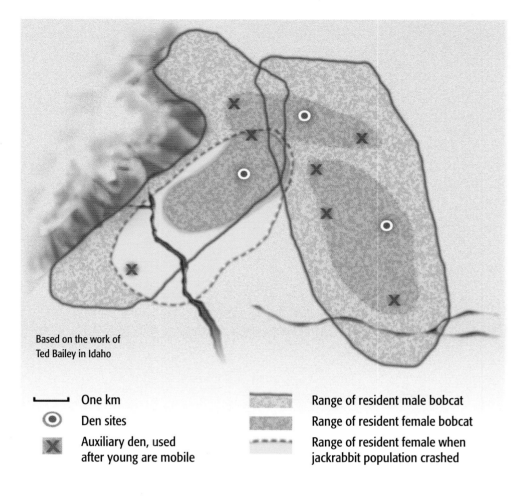

Based on the work of
Ted Bailey in Idaho

| | | |
|---|---|---|
| ⊢——⊣ One km | | ▨ Range of resident male bobcat |
| ◉ Den sites | | ▨ Range of resident female bobcat |
| ✖ Auxiliary den, used after young are mobile | | - - - - - Range of resident female when jackrabbit population crashed |

particular, spend much of their young lives in makeshift beds. For their first three or four days, fawns have all the coordination of a person on 12-foot stilts. When they tire from staggering, they drop—in meadows, in flowerbeds, under alpine fir skirts when the wind is blowing—and rely on their camouflage and relative lack of scent. In the Rockies, I once watched a coyote walk right past a fawn without seeing or smelling it. But a coyote is a restless hunter, always on the move. A bobcat has far more patience. It will sit on a ledge and watch for hours, so it has a greater chance of seeing where a fawn beds down.

But a bobcat doesn't take only newborns. It makes a meal of everything from yearling doe to 150-pound bucks.

*Following spread: A bobcat carries a bobwhite into a thick tangle of brush, where it can eat in peace. Master of the bird and the rabbit, the bobcat is far down in the pecking order of predators and must take steps to protect its catch from wolves, cougars and other interlopers.*

**TWO KILLS WITNESSED**

How does an animal not quite twice the size of a house cat handle a full-grown deer? In 1949, two hunters in New Brunswick witnessed the end of one such encounter. They were walking along a logging road when a deer bolted out of the woods with a bobcat clinging to its shoulder.

63

*Coyotes and wolves are sometimes just curious, but cats
are very goal-oriented. They're there for food, and that's
what it's about.*

—STEVE KNICK

The struggle had been going on for some time, for the
deer was badly winded. It lurched unsteadily along the road
a short distance, then collapsed, "stone-dead." True to their
time, the men fired at the bobcat, but it escaped. When
they examined the deer, they found a jagged hole in its
shoulder that the bobcat had somehow managed to gnaw
during its wild ride.

With smaller prey, the bobcat resorts more to lightning
reflexes than to overpowering stubbornness. Near an Arizona water hole, a biologist watched a bobcat catching bats
at sunset. It either whacked them out of the air with one
quick swat or reared up on its hind legs and clapped both
paws together, the way my old house cat Midnight used to
stun fleeing sparrows. Within half an hour, the bobcat had
caught and eaten about 10 bats.

The bobcat lives more on the fringes of civilization than
does the lynx, but some believe the bobcat is even more
secretive. Perhaps it has simply learned more hard lessons
from humans than its wilderness relative. Although its taste
for the spoils of the barnyard has been greatly exaggerated,
its occasional indulgence has, over the centuries, sent many
a farmer flying out of bed at night, rifle in hand. Theodore
Roosevelt relates how, while he was ranching in North
Dakota, a bobcat "destroyed half my poultry, coming night
after night with most praiseworthy regularity." You have
to admire Roosevelt's good humor. In all the years of our
half-acquaintance with the bobcat's hunting habits, few
farmers have been as charitable.

The opportunistic bob-
cat eats everything
from deer to deer mice.

# CHAPTER 4

# BRIEF ENCOUNTERS

THERE COMES A TIME IN THE LIFE OF EVEN THE MOST SOLI-
tary creature when it must set aside its solitude to mate. For
a few days, the cat's world turns upside down. The silent
predator becomes a screaming banshee. The lonely prowler
takes a constant companion. Eventually, the madness of
estrus subsides, and the male and female go their separate
ways. If the male ever meets his partner in future, it will be
either to mate with her again or, in the case of the cougar,
to kill her or her kittens or both.

In human terms, the male cat is clearly not a support-
ive parent. On the other hand, the female is the ultimate
single mom. Her family responsibilities weigh heaviest
when the young are almost fully grown. In Idaho, a 94-
pound cougar female fed a ravenous threesome of older
kittens weighing 98, 102 and 135 pounds. Such a gang is
able to put away an entire deer at one sitting. Researcher
Martin Jalkotzy believes that all this practice makes female
cats better hunters than males—although with larger prey,
the male's superior size may compensate for the female's
superior experience.

During the early stages of courtship, the female finds a
male's scrape, leaves her own urine like a dropped hankie,
then hangs around, bawling her readiness in a call that "shat-
ters the night and rings through the canyons." The male,
drawn by these hard-to-ignore screams and by the heady
pheromones in the female's urine, homes in. The breeders
are almost always males with territories. A female usually

*In a few short weeks, these two bobcat kittens must learn how to leap, stalk and climb and how to determine what's food, what's danger and what's neutral—all the complex judgments and physical skills they'll need to survive.*

*If you don't see any cat sign, you've got some. If you see some cat sign, you have quite a few. If you see a lot of cat sign, they're everywhere.*

—Steve Knick

*Left: Wide-eyed with wonder, a 4-week-old bobcat investigates everything from a blowing leaf to a beetle trundling by. A kitten's insatiable curiosity quickly lures it beyond the den—sometimes too far. At right, a cougar mother firmly but delicately transports her wayward youngster back to safety.*

mates with only one partner per breeding cycle, but male ranges typically adjoin several female ones, and a male may breed with a number of females. A radio-collared male bobcat in Idaho once divided the night among three partners.

If the male tries to mount before the female is ready, she unequivocally advises him to back off with a swat of her paw. The mating must occur around the peak of her cycle. Each bout lasts just seconds but is repeated up to six times an hour. Cougars may mate 50 to 70 times a day for a week. Those who've watched this behavior in captivity report that after a few hours, the female makes most of the overtures.

The breeding season varies from place to place and from cat to cat. Most bobcat young are born in April and May, after a 62-day gestation period. Lynx often time it so that their young arrive in late May or early June, at the start of the brief northern summer. Cougar births occur mainly during winter in Florida, spring in Idaho, summer in Nevada

*Following spread: Cougar kittens are often rough with each other, but their boisterous play stops short of actual damage, partly because the killing bite is among the last behaviors to mature.*

71

and fall in Wyoming. All northern cats avoid giving birth in midwinter.

The bobcat and lynx share similar family lives, although the lynx prefers to den in the thickest tangle of brush it can find, while the more versatile bobcat may seek out broken rocks or even old beaver lodges. At birth, bobcats weigh a mere 10 to 12 ounces and are blind and helpless. Although they're still pint-sized when they finish nursing two months later, they can already intimidate researchers who try to handle them without precautions, as biologist Steve Knick did once. "It turned into the worst ball of fangs and claws I'd ever seen," he recalls. Bobcat and lynx kittens born early in the summer stay with their mothers until the following spring.

Perhaps the most striking sound you will ever hear in the lonely northern woods is the wail of the mating lynx, "which, for despondency and agony of soul, I have never heard equaled," says naturalist John Burroughs. Cougars

and bobcats have a straightforward alley-cat yowl—as if a heavy rock just fell on their paw—but the lynx's cry resembles emotional anguish more than physical pain. Photographer Tom Kitchin compares it to the moans of "a widow who has just lost her seafaring man in a storm."

Lynx reproduction ebbs and flows not only with the changing seasons but with the phase of the hare cycle. A peak litter of six or seven kittens may drop to three or four during midcycle and even fewer when the hares crash. Of the few kittens born at this time, almost none survive.

Lynx are the grand exception to the rule that North American wild cats do not hunt cooperatively. In the North-

*In a confrontation between a bobcat and a coyote, the cat is all hand speed while the dog is all footwork.*

## WHY DOGS AND CATS CAN'T GET ALONG

In her book *Bobcat Year*, Hope Ryden describes a hypothetical but realistic meeting between a bobcat kitten and a coyote pup. This charming tale of mutual confusion suggests why cats and dogs never have, and never will, see eye to eye:

The bobcat kitten climbed from his lookout rock and slowly advanced toward the coyote pup. In response, the pup hunched and rounded his spine in the manner of a Halloween cat. But this posture, so well understood by coyotes and foxes and, indeed, by most of the world's cats, was not in the bobcat's visual vocabulary. The bobcat expressed aggression by raising his shoulders and presenting not an enlarged view of his side, but his full face, which at maturity would be enhanced by wide muttonchops. In this, he behaved like a maned lion. So the bobcat did not take offense at the coyote's behavior. His mood, in fact, was genial, which could have been easily discerned by another bobcat, for he walked boldly, with his stubby tail held erect.

Now, it was the coyote pup who misread the bobcat's mood. To the coyote, a stiffly held tail signaled hostility. A coyote who wished to communicate friendly intentions did so by carrying his tail in a low, swinging, relaxed position. Accordingly, the pup's hostility now escalated, and he tipped his head to one side, the better to expose his long double row of teeth. But even this exaggerated display did not deter the oncoming kitten, whose unshakable confidence unnerved the coyote. The pup rolled onto his back and assumed a posture of abject submission.

In the more social world of the coyote, this act of surrender would have been understood for what it was—a technique for defusing aggression. The kitten, however, did not understand this conciliatory language. The young bobcat was destined to become a solitary animal whose method of maintaining peace was to avoid other bobcats, so the sociable coyote's sophisticated body language was lost on him. The kitten, in fact, interpreted the coyote's upturned body as an aggressive posture. A warring cat, after all, would flip onto its back to rake an opponent with its hind claws. The kitten, having no means of knowing that the supine creature before him possessed no such weaponry on his hind feet, responded by backing away.

*—adapted from* Bobcat Year *by Hope Ryden, with permission of the author*
*(New York, New York: Lyons & Burford, Publishers, 1981)*

*Quiet moments like this between a female cougar and her 3-week-old kitten become rarer as the kittens get older. A new mother must learn patience as her young practice their hunting skills by catapulting off her head, swatting her on the nose with their needle-sharp claws and even pouncing on her twitching tail.*

west Territories, biologist Kim Poole observed a male and a female together for two months during the nonbreeding time of winter, often within 100 yards of each other. He has also seen tracks of a female and her young fanned out in the snow, the better to flush hares. And in the Yukon, researcher Brian Slough once watched two females crossing a pond with their nine kittens mixed together. If there is not kinship among lynx, there is at least tolerance.

Cougars generally give birth to their one to six (usually two or three) kittens in a rock crevice or a thick matrix of underbrush. Newborn kittens are blind and spotted and have exotically ringed tails. In about 10 days, their startling blue eyes open to the world. At that point, they may try to wobble around, but it is usually another few days before a measure of coordination replaces slapstick cuteness. After half a year, the kittens' sky-blue eyes change to a murky hazel and the baby spots begin to fade.

For the first six to eight weeks, the kittens remain at the den, chugging on their mother's milk and indulging

*Early one spring, as wilderness guide Bob Sutherland and a friend were hiking in British Columbia's Strathcona Provincial Park, a cougar crossed the trail just ahead of them. When they reached the tracks it had left in the snow, they found a picture postcard of a cougar lying face up on the trail. "It was as if it had left its business card," says Sutherland.*

in kittenlike antics. Cougars are hard-wired to recognize deer as prey, but the ability to bring them down consistently is an acquired art. The 18 to 24 months that the kittens spend with their mother is therefore an important apprenticeship. That apprenticeship begins early: One California female was seen bringing live grasshoppers to her month-old kittens for practice.

After about two months, the mother begins leading her kittens to the larger prey she has killed. Here, they eat and reenact the motions of the catch. The cougar is one mother that does not discourage her young from playing with their food. The mother-kitten vocabulary is not well documented, but it does include that universal parental command, "Come here." From tracks in the snow, Martin Jalkotzy once deduced that a mother had headed for home after a successful hunt. Two hundred yards from the den, she had apparently summoned her kittens to join her so that the family could return to the kill site together.

Sometimes, 9 out of 10 kittens reach adulthood; sometimes, only 1 out of 10. Survival depends mainly on whether the mother is killed prematurely by hunters and on how cannibalistic the local male cougars are.

Researchers believe that the family breaks up when the mother abandons the grown-up kittens at a kill site, and they disperse in search of a territory. Young immigrant males may wander a modest 30 miles or so, but sometimes, they travel completely out of their home district. These great roamers fill a vital role: Each local population needs at least one immigrant per generation to remain genetically healthy.

Immigrants sometimes take over a range on the death of its owner, or they may claim small footholds and expand them through territorial "discussions" with aging neighbors. A young female breeds for the first time at about 2½ years of age, males at about 3 years. By then, both have long put aside their wobbly kittenlike ways and have acquired the grave and dignified demeanor of a major predator.

*The newly opened eyes of a cougar kitten are as blue as a mountain sky, but they fade to a murky hazel by about 6 months.*

# CHAPTER 5

# MAN AND CAT

FOR MANY, THE WILD CAT SYMBOLIZES THE SPIRIT OF IN-
dependence, but historically, it was not a favorite with the
rugged individualists who settled North America. That
antipathy was not necessarily aimed at wild cats in particular but was, instead, part of a general attitude toward all
predators. Today, it is hard to understand why any sane
rancher would want to shoot a wild cat on sight, but when
a pioneer family with two cows to its name lost both to a
mountain lion, it's easy to see how a certain them-or-us
mentality might have developed.

Not only was the cougar forced to endure persecution,
but like the wolf, it was considered cowardly for trying to
escape its persecutors. In 1709, North Carolina historian
John Lawson wrote contemptuously about how "the least
Cur" could tree a cougar. Two centuries later, that con-
tempt had not diminished. In the early 1900s, professional
hunter John Goff declared that of the 300 cougars he had
killed, only two had "fought courageously." Ironically,
the same people who proclaimed the cougar cowardly
often told hair-raising stories of their own bravery in the
face of this "fierce" adversary.

*In one two-month
period, a rancher in
California lost 175
chickens and 40 pigs
to a bobcat. Although
rare, such incidents led
pioneers to declare war
on all predators.*

**FIRST CONTACT** Because of their shyness, wild cats were something of a
mystery even to native peoples. Wolves figure in tribal
legends 20 times more often than do cougars, and bobcats
and lynx are even more marginal. Where the cats do appear in myths, it is often in the last sentence or two of a

seemingly unrelated tale. "Origin of the Lynx" (page 91) is a perfect example.

Yet scattered here and there, like faint paw prints, are traces of the cats' mark on the aboriginals of North America. Some desert tribes of the Southwest openly revered the cougar. In part, that was because they obtained their meat from scavenging cougar kills, and in part, it was because chance sightings happen more often in the desert, as scientists Ken Logan and Linda Sweanor discovered in New Mexico. Seeing a cougar would surely have been as significant an event for the ancient Hopi as it is for us.

Tokens of the cats showed up in the rituals of these Southwestern tribes. Many fashioned ornamental quivers out of cougar skin. Since cougars seemed to give birth without trouble, the Apaches used the skin in maternity belts. Others applied bobcat tenderloin to cure headaches.

Attitudes in the northern forests were different. Pacific Northwest tribes didn't like the cougar. And in the Yukon, Tlingit hunters viewed the lynx as a powerful, somewhat

*Guns and traps have exacted a heavy toll on cougars, bobcats and lynx over the years, but their greatest enemy by far is the bulldozer.*

82

## WHY THE COUGAR IS LONG AND LEAN

A long time ago, Cougar was a short, thickset person. He was always a great thief, but once he went too far. One day, Old Man, the Great Trickster, had caught and roasted some Squirrel-people. He was ravenous, as usual, but his catch was so big that he couldn't finish eating it. So he laid the remaining Squirrels on a willow plate and fell asleep.

When he awoke, the Squirrels were gone. Old Man's sharp eyes soon spotted a trail in the grass where Cougar had walked with those soft paws of his. "Aha," said Old Man, "Cougar has stolen my Squirrels. But I'll find him, for I made him and know all his ways."

Old Man followed Cougar's trail up hill and over dale, until at last, he came to a place where the grass was all bent down. There, he found his willow plate—empty.

Soon, Old Man found Cougar himself, asleep atop a big stone. He crept up carefully, for Cougars are much faster than men. When he was close enough, he grabbed the thief by the tail. It wasn't much of a tail then, but enough to hold onto.

"I'll show you," he said. "Steal from the man who made you, you night-prowling rascal!"

Old Man put his foot behind Cougar's head and pulled Cougar's body so hard that it stretched out long and thin. Then he pulled Cougar's tail till it became almost as long as Cougar's body. "Now you are too long and lean to get fat," said Old Man. "And that is how you and your children will always look."

*—from the Chippewa of the Northwest*

malevolent spirit and, out of caution, always pretended that a trapped one had been caught by accident.

Early mentions of the mountain lion by white explorers in the 15th and 16th centuries were brief and neutral. Amerigo Vespucci was the first to record a sighting in the western hemisphere, off the coast of Nicaragua. Cabeza de Vaca spotted the first one in North America, near the Everglades. But casual observation changed to hostility not long after the newcomers left their ships. In the 1500s, Jesuit priests in California offered local natives a bull for every cougar they killed. Some states used more direct coercion: A 1695 South Carolina statute forced every aboriginal to kill a cougar or a wolf or a bear or two bobcats each year or to endure a public flogging.

## THE FURRED DEMON

Around the same time, states like Connecticut began paying bounties for cougars. Not content with sporadic results, many eventually hired professional bounty hunters. Of these, none was more dedicated than Ben Lilly, who plied his trade around the turn of this century, first in lower Mississippi River country, then in Arizona and New Mexico. Lilly saw himself not so much as a hunter but as a vampire slayer; he believed he was doing God's work by exorcising furred demons from the land. With a zealot's passion, he tracked down bears and cougars, boasting that he never saw a cougar he wasn't at least able to wound. He was "a notionless sort of feller," according to his biographer, J. Frank Dobie. As a youth, Lilly honed his aim by shooting mosquitoes with a .22-caliber rifle. He ate panther neck meat for its supposed strength-giving properties and used panther oil to temper his eccentrically shaped knives. An inveterate walker, Lilly wore out a pair of boots every two weeks until he started reinforcing the soles with strips of old auto tires. A pair of these double-soled clodhoppers weighed just under 12 pounds. As a further refinement, he cut holes in the sides of the boots "to let the water out." In his career, Lilly killed about 600 cougars, including nine in one "good" week in 1914.

Lilly was the most colorful of the wildlife executioners, but he was not the only member of his trade. Altogether, about 80,000 cougars have been killed in this century. The bounties may be gone, but all western provinces and states except California still allow cougar hunting. In Texas, the cat can be shot anytime, anywhere, in any number. In some quarters, at least, the old pioneer war on predators still rages.

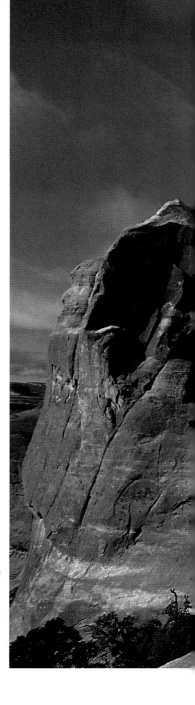

**THE CRIME OF CRIMES**

Although we no longer believe that cougars "lure brave men to destruction by simulating the cry of a woman in distress," they do quietly stalk people on rare occasions. In North America, only the polar bear shares that ominous distinction.

In the past 100 years, there have been 15 fatal and about 50 nonfatal cougar attacks. To put this into perspective, 100 people die each year when their vehicles crash into white-tailed deer on our highways. A person is 20 times more likely to die from a black widow spider bite and 650 times more likely to be killed by lightning than to be killed by a cougar. Even for those who hike regularly in cougar coun-

*In search of the 6,000 calories she needs every day, a female cougar patrols a spectacular Utah archscape.*

try, an attack is not so much a risk as a freak occurrence.

North America's first known cougar victim was probably Philip Tanner, whose intriguing tombstone still stands in a quiet country cemetery in Lewisville, Pennsylvania. On May 6, 1751, the 58-year-old millwright was killed at the edge of a nearby woods. In those days, it was the custom to chisel an image of the cause of demise on the gravestone. Whoever carved Tanner's marker was no Michelangelo, but the crude figure does seem to be a crouching cougar, its long tail arched over its back. Another headstone in the same cemetery bears the Four of Diamonds—presumably marking the grave

85

*Its white teeth glistened with portentous rage.*

—Cyrus Roys

of a gambler who may have played one hand too many.

Of the 65 recorded cougar attacks, many have happened in the past 20 years. As cougar populations rose after the cat's reclassification from "varmint" to semiprotected game animal, more cougars began to live in ever-dwindling wilderness areas, and more people than ever began to explore that wilderness.

Well over half of the cougar's victims—about 40—have been children. One child had stooped to tie a shoe; another was bending over to look at tadpoles in a pond. It does seem that a child in a vulnerable situation occasionally triggers predatory behavior. Zoo officials admit that kids often send cougars into the stalk-and-pounce mode. A photographer I know who brought his 11-year-old niece

*Cougar attacks are rare, but as wilderness shrinks and more people crowd into the little that remains, they are on the increase.*

## HOW NOT TO BECOME A COUGAR VICTIM

You're more likely to be killed by falling airplane parts than by a cougar, but "it is impossible to reduce this small risk to zero without eliminating either cougars or humans from cougar habitat," points out Paul Beier, one of North America's premier cougar researchers. "Neither is acceptable."

Some state and provincial governments have published pamphlets outlining how to avoid attacks in cougar country and how to handle yourself in the unlikely event of a cougar confrontation. Among the tips offered are:

• If a cougar attacks, fight back with rocks, sticks, fists, anything. The "play dead" advice that is often ingrained in hikers in grizzly country is not the way to handle a big cat. Here, playing dead might quickly become a permanent condition.

• If you run into a grizzly, it's often wise to avert your eyes, as a submissive gesture. With an approaching cougar, however, clamp your eyes on the cat's eyes and never take them away.

• Upon sighting a cougar, immediately lift children off the ground.

• Since projectiles and swinging objects such as sticks or tripods are not found in nature, their use might successfully discourage an aggressive cougar.

• Don't run or turn your back on a cougar.

• Never approach a cougar, especially one at a kill or with kittens.

• Shout, wave your arms, do anything to bluff the cat into believing you're bigger and more powerful than you are.

to visit a captive but uncaged cougar eventually had to put the girl in the car, because the usually docile cat took such a disturbingly intense interest in her.

Sometimes, the offending cougar is what one researcher calls "a dumb adolescent" that hasn't yet learned to hunt deer or elk consistently. Sometimes, the cat simply makes a mistake: It tries to take down a horse, for instance, and there happens to be someone on it. Sometimes, the victim is jogging or mountain biking—behaviors which a predator may interpret as fleeing and which may prompt it to give chase. Perhaps the person is kneeling down for a drink of water, placing his or her neck within easy reach. "A human standing up is just not the right shape for a cat's prey," says longtime cougar researcher John Seidensticker.

Yet we often forget that animals are individuals, and it's impossible to generalize about how an entire species behaves. Seidensticker himself has had one close call that had nothing to do with crouching, jogging, kids or dumb adolescent cats. He was tracking a radio-collared female in a lodgepole pine forest when the sharp bark of a nearby squirrel alerted him to the cougar, which stood about 60 feet away, peering from behind a lodgepole pine. She hissed,

*Bloodcurdling tales about marauding cougars made great newspaper fare throughout the 1800s. One such epic described a communal hunt in which a cougar seemed to be pitted against an entire district. The beleaguered cat reportedly survived fights with dogs, a broken leg, five bullets in the head, stabbings from pocketknives "and other assorted cudgelings." Despite such extraordinary endurance, cougars were rarely considered courageous.*

laid her ears back and started coming toward him. Seidensticker yelled, but the cougar kept advancing. At that point, she was a mere 30 feet away.

The biologist glanced down briefly to pick up a thick limb from the ground. But the cougar took advantage of that momentary loss of eye contact to halve the distance between them. Taking nervous aim, he threw the stick and hit her on the shoulder. She left.

Seidensticker usually carries a gun when tracking cougars, not for protection but to bag the occasional grouse for supper. That day, he'd left it at home—a blessing in disguise. This female was the most important subject in his study, but if he'd had the gun with him that day, he says, he would have shot her; it was that close.

*Often near but rarely seen, a cougar slips silently past a Montana ranch house.*

88

## WHAT'S IN A NAME?

Although pioneers may have slaughtered wild cats at every opportunity, they also acknowledged their mystique by naming hundreds of mountains, creeks, lakes, islands, bayous, knolls and keys after them. In the United States, 3,206 geographic features bear the name of one of the three cats. Although "wildcat" is the most popular single moniker (appearing 984 times), names using the many common names for *Puma concolor* combine to make it by far the most celebrated cat overall. All but six states have a Catamount Creek, a Panther Bluff or some other lionized feature.

Canada has 238 feline place names. Appropriately, the lynx is the overall favorite, at 84. There would have been 85, but in modern times, Lynx Lake in Quebec was renamed Lac Ventadour. Here, the cat was a victim not of trapping but of politics.

The most famous feline place in North America is the Catskill Mountains—those rolling hills that serve as a weekend wilderness for so many New Yorkers. The name comes from *Kaaters Kill*, which is Dutch for Wildcat Creek.

## GRAND ATTACK CENTRAL

More than 20 attacks have occurred in the past 100 years on Vancouver Island, off the coast of British Columbia. Near the west-coast village of Tofino, rural kids learn about cougars just as urban kids are streetproofed and schoolchildren in Los Angeles practice earthquake drills. Sometimes, though, nothing can prepare you for a cougar attack. In January 1951, a cougar crashed through the window of an isolated cabin on the island and seized the lone occupant, a telephone lineman. The man fought his way into the kitchen, grabbed a knife and stabbed the cat. He then ran out into the winter night in his underwear, hopped into his boat and motored six miles to a neighbor's cabin, where he phoned for help.

Pioneer cougar researcher Maurice Hornocker has speculated that the 800 cougars on Vancouver Island are more aggressive than other populations, but wildlife officials in British Columbia have a simpler explanation. Deer may be a cougar's main prey, but throughout most of its range, the cougar also takes smaller animals—something that is all but absent on Vancouver Island. To make matters worse, many deer and elk prefer to browse the fresh forage of the island's many clear-cut hillsides. This paucity of cover makes big-game hunting virtually impossible for the cougar. It must be tempting for the cats to establish themselves near the only small prey on the island—the dogs and cats and raccoons around towns. In fact, most of the attacks on people have taken place in these locations rather than in wilderness areas.

## HOW THE BOBCAT GOT ITS SPOTS

The first man in the world was Saynday. He was tall and thin, with a droopy pencil mustache. He created everything. One day, the ever hungry Saynday was making some meat soup by putting hot stones into a pool with meat in it. The soup was almost ready when he realized he'd forgotten his spoon. Bobcat, sitting in a tree overlooking the pond, offered to guard the soup till Saynday returned.

But Bobcat, like Saynday himself, was tricky, and the minute the man left, Bobcat lapped up almost all the soup. Just a little remained in the bottom.

When Saynday returned, he wept long and hard over his lost meal. Then he saw the reflection of Bobcat, who was still in the tree above the pond. "There's the bad one who ate up all my soup," he cried and began throwing stones at Bobcat's reflection. He threw harder and harder, until the soup and mud splashed up and spotted Bobcat's fur. "There," said Saynday, "you can wear those spots for always, to show people what a soup-stealer you are."

—from the Kiowa of the Great Plains

*Bobcats and lynx are rare in native American folklore and imagery, but a few legends have survived. In parts of Alaska, for example, it was considered bad luck to leave the bones from a trapped lynx on the trail. They all had to be thrown into the fire.*

## ORIGIN OF THE LYNX

Once there was a blind man and his wife. Before he lost his sight, the man had been a great hunter, but now he and his wife were on the verge of starvation. One autumn, the two of them went to a creek where the woman caught spawning salmon.

Suddenly, she saw a large black bear come down to the creek to fish. When she told her husband, he was so excited by the prospect of the hunt that he asked her to fetch his bow and arrow. As he felt the bow string tighten beneath his fingers, he almost forgot he was blind. He let fly the arrow, which struck the bear and killed it instantly, without a sound. But his wife lied and told him he missed, because she wanted all the meat for herself. Later, she slipped away, skinned the animal and began boiling the flesh in a large pot.

"I smell fresh-killed meat," said the blind man.

"What are you talking about?" mocked the greedy wife. "You can't shoot."

When she slipped away again to tend to her cooking, a supernatural being who had seen the blind man's misfortunes took pity on him and restored his sight. As the man looked around, amazed at his good luck, he saw his wife bending over the pot with the bear meat. She was hungrily eating the fat that she had skimmed from the surface of the water. He was so angry at her meanness that he crept up behind her and threw her into the boiling pot. Then he tore her clothing, her flesh, even her bones, into small pieces and scattered them in all directions. Each fragment became a lynx, and they were the ancestors of all lynx.

*—from the Bellacoola of British Columbia*

# TWO MODERN CAT TALES

## FLORIDA PANTHER: THE GLAMOUR PUSS

THE FLORIDA PANTHER BELONGS TO THE RARE ECHELON OF animal celebrities. Its haunted eyes gaze at us from magazine covers, T-shirts and postage stamps. There are Florida panther societies, the Florida Panther Wildlife Refuge, even a Florida Panthers hockey team. It is the state animal. Several books and hundreds of articles have been written about it. There's a one-year waiting list for journalists who want to accompany panther researchers on their rounds.

Yet the Florida panther (*Puma concolor coryi*) is just one of 29 living subspecies of cougar spanning North and South America. A subspecies is a population that is different from other populations in some way. Island and peninsula subspecies tend to be more distinct than mainland ones. Although it's hard to generalize from so few specimens, the Florida panther is usually described as slightly darker than other cougar populations, with longer legs and a broad, flat nose. Originally, an estimated 2,000 to 3,400 roamed from Florida west to Texas and north to Tennessee. Today, 30 to 50 adults and about as many kittens shakily cling to existence in southern Florida.

Two formidable problems stand between the Florida panther and survival. The first is habitat loss. Florida's pleasant climate makes this global epidemic more acute than usual, because everyone from orange growers to retiring snowbirds wants a little piece of the Sunshine State. The second problem is more insidious: Because of its small population and decades of isolation, the Florida panther has

*The Florida panther is too inbred to survive, so biologists have introduced another subspecies from nearby Texas in the hope that the hybrids will have fewer birth defects. Says one researcher: "The study of the Florida panther is already the study of history."*

## THE HYBRID SOLUTION

*In the end, they won't save the Florida panther, but they may save the panther in Florida.*

—JOHN SEIDENSTICKER

become a case of classic inbreeding. Ongoing research on DNA fingerprinting—a technique for comparing the hereditary makeup of different individuals—has shown that Florida panthers have almost no genetic variation. The panthers' DNA "looks like bar codes on identical cans of tomatoes," according to Melody Roelke, the researcher who helped uncover the cat's incestuous heritage.

## THE OLD FLORIDA

A few years ago, I spent an unforgettable afternoon in the heart of Florida panther country. It was near the end of a two-week 4,500-mile whirlwind trip around the state. I'd tried to hit all the visual highs and lows, from the roseate spoonbills of Mrazek Pond to those ineffably tacky mini-golf theme parks. Both, in their own way, seemed so "Florida." On this particular afternoon, I was driving along Highway 41—one of the asphalt corridors bridging the Atlantic and Gulf coasts—when I noticed an interesting view off the side of the road and pulled over. It was Faka-hatchee Strand. A strand is really just a thick swamp, but the tall grass, laced with blackwater creeks, looked warm and inviting in the afternoon light.

Assembling my folding kayak, I launched it into one of the creeks. Part of the dark back of a water moccasin, thick as the sweet spot on a baseball bat, surfaced before submerging in reptilian slow motion. As I paddled deeper into the swamp, flanked by 10-foot walls of intensely green grass, little alligators and bugs skittered madly out of the way. (I was later told that alligators had forged these channels.) Innumerable side streams beckoned to be explored. It was a labyrinth, and I had to keep careful track of how many left turns I made and how many right. Time and again, something invisible thrashed in the water at my approach. Finally, one of the creeks opened into a wide, shallow pond populated by several surprised cranes and about 500 ducks that exploded upward in a cloud as they spotted the drifting kayak. They circled above me and filled the

*A thick patch of palmettos is a favored den site of the endangered Florida panther.*

air with the loud flap of their wings. It was like a scene from Alfred Hitchcock's thriller *The Birds*, only calming.

Though I was at most a quarter of a mile from the road, the thickness of the swamp and the abundance of wildlife made it seem as if I'd traveled through a time portal into the 16th-century Florida of Cabeza de Vaca—a Florida that stretched on forever, mazelike and mysterious. Even the world-class bird life of the Anhinga Trail and Sanibel Island that I'd admired earlier in the trip had not had this magic.

Fakahatchee Strand is one of the last bastions of the Florida panther. The meager population is divided among Everglades National Park, Big Cypress National Preserve

*The Florida panther is so inbred that it's pushing the biological limit of what's possible.*

—MELODY ROELKE

and Fakahatchee Strand. While it may be great country for ducks, it is marginal, at best, for the Florida panther. Few cougars in North America have ever had to put up with a boggier, more parasite-infested, unproductive home. Ironically, the saving grace of these glades has been that very inhospitality. Over the past 100 years, they have provided a refuge from human incursion and human persecution.

But Fakahatchee Strand is no longer neglected or inaccessible. Three major highways crisscross the swamps. Oil has been discovered in Big Cypress. Of the estimated 3,500 square miles of panther habitat, half is on private land— mostly large cattle ranches. As the number of immigrants to Florida hits 300,000 a year, some of these ranches are becoming subdivisions. Others fall to "the citrus enemy": Orange growers have a new fondness for the South because the chances of killer frosts ruining the harvest are less. But every new orange grove represents a total loss for the panthers.

Fearing that the presence of this four-legged celebrity may compromise their right to do with their land as they please, many ranchers will not allow biologists on their property to study the cats. Currently, only 22 panthers are radio-collared and monitored.

CLONES Even in healthy populations, it seems that the farther down a peninsula you go, the more the genetic diversity decreases. Those living at the very end have one toe permanently dipped in evolutionary danger. Sometime after 1900, when the Florida panther became a remnant population isolated from its nearest neighbors, that dipped toe became totally immersed.

Historically, the Florida panther had exchanged genes with bordering subspecies of the Texas, midwestern and eastern cougar populations, but as decades passed and litter after litter of kittens grew up to breed with their fathers and mothers and each other, the inevitable came to pass.

With no infusion of fresh genes from outside, the Florida panther became a population of near clones. Geneticist Dr. Stephen O'Brien compares it to more than half a dozen generations of human siblings mating.

The Florida panther also suffers from a litany of other woes—too little land, too many cars, too few deer, hogs carrying lethal viruses and raccoons laced with mercury—but the inbreeding situation has proved the most critical. In wild animals, you never see the genetic disasters—"If you have three legs and two heads, you just don't make it out of the nest," says Melody Roelke—but the less obvious problems are bad enough: holes in the heart; conditions that might indicate weakened immune systems; and most of all, reproductive failure. Ninety-four percent of Florida panther sperm is abnormally formed. Of 23 pregnancies that Roelke observed, only 10 offspring survived beyond 6 months of age. And the problem was worsening with each new generation. Florida panthers were on the fast track to extinction.

A three-toed snail with half those problems would be extinct by now. But the Florida panther was "charismatic megafauna"—a long-tailed pop star—so money and manpower were available. Biologists and government agencies scrambled for a solution. They built 36 highway underpasses at almost a million dollars apiece to reduce panther road-kill. After much debate and over the objections of those who consider the genetic peril overblown, they also

decided to crossbreed the remaining Florida panthers with the Texas subspecies, *Puma concolor stanleyana*. This would further compromise the Florida subspecies, but the hope of ensuring genetic purity had probably already disappeared 40 years ago. In any case, the neighboring populations did interbreed now and then under natural circumstances. In 1995, the first batch of eight Texas females was released. By the end of 1996, four litters of Texas/Florida hybrids had been born.

In 1988, biologists carried out the first of two temporary reintroductions of Texas cats to northern Florida to see whether cougars could live elsewhere in the state. This first attempt did not go well. Three of the seven cats died within a year. The others strayed too close to civilization and, in the end, were prematurely shipped back to Texas. From 1993 to 1995, they tried it again in northern Florida with 10 cougars. Although this went better, there were still a few too many sightings. To minimize public resistance, the hope is to introduce a phan-

*Cougars, bobcats and lynx are most active around dawn and dusk, which can make reliable identification difficult. In deceptive terrain, it's sometimes hard to tell whether you've just glimpsed a cougar at 200 feet or a house cat at 60 feet.*

*I was surprised at its great size and apparent strength. It gave one a new idea of our American forests and the vigor of nature here. It was evident that it could level a platoon of men with a stroke of its paw.*

—HENRY DAVID THOREAU
*(on seeing a cougar skin and skull in Vermont in 1856)*

tom cat like the ones in southern Florida that almost no one ever sees. From the outset, saving the Florida panther has been a delicate political dance more than a flat-out race.

Theoretically, several places in Florida can still support a modest number of cougars. Unfortunately, a healthy self-sustaining population needs at least 500 breeding individuals, and even if some refuges could be linked like beads on a string, there is just not enough space left for that many panthers. Their current habitat will not hold much more than 50, which means that as long as it survives, the Florida panther will have to remain on genetic life support. In a sense, it will be much like those ailing retired folks who need regular prescription renewals to continue soaking up the Florida sunshine.

## EASTERN COUGAR: A UFO WITH PAWS

While the Florida panther struggles with inbreeding and habitat loss, the main problem associated with the eastern cougar is proof of its existence. Throughout eastern North America, reports of a large cat with a long tail crop up with the regularity of sightings of the Loch Ness monster. Some biologists have even dubbed the sightings UFOs— Unidentified Furry Objects.

In my home city of Toronto, Canada—one of the least likely cougar habitats on the continent—recent sightings in one suburb made the evening news for several days running. Although I winced when I saw the dog paw print that some television cameraman had decided to pass off as a mysterious track, one of the witnesses sounded credible enough that I gave him a call. Jim Jodouin is a supervisor of security and safety at Metro Toronto Zoo, so you'd expect him to know a cougar from a tabby or a Great Dane. His description was totally convincing, although the later testimony of others in the neighborhood who claimed to have seen "slinky shadows in the bushes" was somewhat less so. Still, there was no hard evidence, and interest soon petered out. This was, after all, just another one of 400 sightings in Ontario since 1935.

The eastern cougar (*Puma concolor couguar*) was never common in the East, but it did exist from South Carolina north to New Brunswick and west to the Mississippi. The cause of its disappearance in the late 1800s is a clue to its status today.

The case of Vermont is typical. The last known Vermont cougar was shot on Thanksgiving Day 1881 near the town of Barnard. Cougars, even dead ones, were such a sensation in those days that the hunters stuffed the animal and exhibited it around the state, charging 10 cents for the privilege of viewing this "King of the Brute Creation." You can still see the famous Barnard cougar today. By now sun-bleached and frayed around the edges, it snarls at visitors from its glass booth in the foyer of the Vermont Historical Society Museum in Montpelier. Since it stands in the foyer, the curious no longer need to pay even 10 cents to see it.

Barnard itself is a small town plunked in the middle of Vermont's lovely Green Mountains. Ironically, "No Hunting" signs now post the woods where the legendary cougar was shot. As I gazed out one late-October day over the rich forests, still bronzed with the fall color of oak and beech trees, I could imagine cougars living in those thick stands today. There are plenty of white-tailed deer for food and lots of rough country in which to hide.

**THE CASE AGAINST** What is not apparent to the visitor, however, is that like most of New England, the Green Mountains were not always so green. We tend to regard our era as the low point in wilderness history, but over much of the East, things were worse 150 years ago. Today, forests cover more than 82 percent of Vermont, for example, but in 1850, only 25 percent of the state was wooded. People—hunters, pioneers—lived on what now appear to be virgin slopes. Wellholes and stone walls still dot the forested hillsides. By the end of the Civil War, when many of the mountain

100

*The debate over the eastern cougar's existence may have a surprising conclusion: Preliminary genetic tests of old museum skins suggest that there is no difference between the original eastern cougar and the western subspecies, above.*

people migrated west, there was scarcely a deer anywhere in Vermont. It was so bad that in 1878, Vermont introduced 17 deer from New York State, which itself was only slightly better off. These imported deer founded the healthy population of 120,000 that exists today.

So while the cougar had a price on its head throughout the East, it wasn't just the bounty that did it in. For about 40 years, its main prey was virtually extirpated from eastern North America. If the cats retreated deeper into the woods, as some biologists have hopefully speculated, it's uncertain what they could have eaten. Unlike Florida, the Northeast did not have large

*The cat has an extra organ in the roof of its mouth that is especially sensitive to sex hormones. When a cat grimaces as if in distaste, it is "sniffing" with this organ—a gesture known as flehmen. At the end of the grimace, it often licks its lips.*

numbers of alternative prey, such as armadillos and wild hogs.

Nowadays, prey would not be a problem. There are 25 million white-tailed deer in North America, which is more than there were when the Pilgrims landed. In winter, the deer congregate in "yards"—treed areas between 20 and 8,000 acres in size. In Vermont, spruce and balsam stands are especially popular. Thick spruce tops catch the snow, which sublimates without falling to the ground. In one study, the depth of snow in a spruce stand was 8 inches, compared with 43 inches in the open fields and 32 inches in the sugar bush.

To an animal like the deer, which supports a relatively heavy body on toothpick legs, the yard brings welcome relief from plodding through chest-deep snow. While in the yard, however, deer are easy pickings for predators. Coyote and bobcat tracks are a common sight in these areas. But no one has ever seen signs of a cougar.

Despite their intelligence, cats are as naive as other animals when it comes to crossing roads. In Florida, before wildlife underpasses were built in the late 1980s, car fenders were one of the most common causes of panther mortality. Although there were only three dozen Florida cats in existence, their presence was obvious—not from sightings but from road-kills. Similarly, when New York tried to reintroduce lynx into the Adirondacks in the early 1990s, at least a quarter died on the Interstate within two years. Yet not one eastern cougar has ever turned up as road-kill.

## THE CASE FOR

That's not to say no hard cougar evidence has been found. A small number of cougars have been shot in the East, not only earlier in this century but in the past few years. In 1994, scat found near Craftsbury, Vermont, was analyzed by a forensics lab and found to contain cougar fur, presumably from grooming. There are also accounts from reliable eyewitnesses such as Toronto's Jim Jodouin.

However, the real question is not whether there are

cougars in the East but where these individuals come from. Most important, is there a breeding population?

It's almost certain that the answer to the last question is no. As for all the sightings over the years—20 to 30 annually in many eastern states and provinces—I think of the books of Charles Fort. In the early years of this century, Fort tirelessly accumulated reports of thousands of unidentified flying objects, hailstorms of frogs and other peculiar celestial events. The closets of his Brooklyn flat were stacked high with shoeboxes full of index cards to the supernatural. In works like *The Book of the Damned*, he good-humoredly offered this avalanche of research as food for thought. Most of these UFOs may well be weather balloons, he reasoned, but if only one isn't... what then?

Likewise, many cougar sightings have been traced to everything from cows and skunks to a cardboard box blowing across the road. Even real cats, perhaps more than UFOs, have an uncanny ability to play tricks on the eyes. Biologist Gerry Parker was once tracking a radio-collared lynx— a 28-pound female—beside a Nova Scotia logging road. Suddenly, she emerged from the forest, looked both ways, then crossed the road ahead of him and disappeared into the woods on the other side. "My first thought was, what a big cat!" he recalls. "Then I thought of recent cougar sightings in the Maritimes, and my memory started playing tricks. Did what I see have a long tail? Was it tawny-colored? Soon, I was no longer sure of anything. I could easily have made that lynx into an 80-pound tawny cat with a long tail."

Many witnesses weaken their case by claiming to have seen "black panthers." The melanistic phase of *Puma concolor* has never turned up in North America, yet in some places, as many as one sighting in four describes the cat as black.

Still, once you've eliminated all the cardboard boxes and house cats seen from deceptive distances, you're left with a core of real cougar sightings. These animals may have wandered from the nearest established population—after all, some

radio-collared western cats have roamed more than 300 miles. A few of the eastern cougars from the 1930s, 1940s and 1950s may have been such individuals. Nowadays, however, the nearest cougars to the Northeast are in the Black Hills of South Dakota and the strands of southern Florida. Florida panthers have not even managed to spread to the northern portion of their state, let alone travel 1,000 miles through some of the most developed parts of the continent.

A far likelier scenario is that the genuine sightings are pets released in the woods. Many northeastern states allow pet cougars—Pennsylvania, for example, has 48 registered cougars; Massachusetts has 250—and some biologists

107

In parts of New England, radical environmental groups have been accused of releasing pet cougars in the hope that the presence of an "eastern cougar" would force the government to set aside land for their survival under the Endangered Species Act.

*A rocky area makes a perfect day bed for the cougar. On cold days, it can bask in the warmth of the sun reflecting off the rocks, while on hot days, it can retreat to the shade of a small grotto.*

speculate that the number of unregistered cats is about three times the number of registered ones. It's easy to imagine that some irresponsible buyers, swayed by the cuteness of a cougar kitten, have second thoughts when the kitten matures into a 150-pound predator in the basement. There are several cases of released exotics living for years—even a chimpanzee that escaped from a circus in late winter managed to survive at least half a year in Michigan's Upper Peninsula. If a chimpanzee can make it, surely a cougar can. The released-pet theory gained further credibility when a cougar shot in Quebec in 1992 was found to have Chilean genes.

Despite the long odds, many people still believe that a natural population of eastern cougars exists in the Northeast. Almost every state and province has a Charles Fort with a predilection for amassing data on cougar sightings. These people find strength in the sheer number of records. They point out that the coyote, long dismissed by earlier generations of government biologists, is now an accepted presence in the East. As for hard proof of wild cats, they rightly maintain that absence of evidence is not necessarily evidence of absence. In the end, the eastern cougar's existence seems to be mainly an article of faith.

I must confess that I have a hard time believing in either UFOs or eastern cougars. Although I understand the eagerness of the believers, I keep remembering what naturalist Ted Levin told me when I visited him at his home in Thetford, Vermont. Levin had recently returned from three weeks of tracking panthers in Florida with biologists. Despite the radio-collars and the expert company, however, he never even glimpsed a cat. "In Florida, they have 50 cats, and no one sees them," says Levin. "In Vermont, we have no cats, and everyone sees them."

But later that day, as I looked over the Green Mountains outside Barnard, so thick with trees and deer and promise, one thought warmed me: Cougars may not be there now, but they *can* be.

# FELINE FUTURES

THE LAST GREAT MYSTERY OF OUR WILD CATS IS THEIR future. These days, most of us wish them well, and that's been a real awakening. Calls for extermination now ring only from the fringes. But even as the sounds of gunfire and the snap of leg-hold traps become fainter, the roar of bulldozers grows louder. For top predators like cats, it may signal the final battle. You can legislate hunting and trapping with the stroke of a pen, but there's no easy answer to loss of wilderness. If wild cats are to continue far into the next millennium, one or two more mass awakenings will have to occur quickly.

There are three discomfiting problems, and they're about us. The first is arithmetic: A country can't double its population every 50 years without turning millions of square miles of forest into subdivisions. It's tempting to dismiss overpopulation and overdevelopment as having to do with the other guy, but it also includes the nature-loving couple whose dream is a modest house backing onto a small woods or a brook. North America is so overdeveloped that we're competing with wildlife for every remaining stream and patch of forest. Usually, we never even hear the trees fall. Developers do the dirty work, and we move in with a clear conscience. But if permits for dream homes were suddenly denied and we had to start building vertically instead of horizontally, wild cats might lose many of their current supporters.

The second problem is economics: To those who

*Alaska and Canada still have plenty of lynx, but only 300 to 650 remain in the Lower 48—mostly in Idaho, Washington, Maine and Montana. To survive, the lynx will need to be protected under the Endangered Species Act.*

accept the human-centered world-view, stewardship of nature means harvesting it for our benefit. That includes cutting forests, mining slopes and damming rivers. In a battle between the board of directors that wants another year of 15 percent profits for its shareholders and the cougar that's just looking to survive, it's easy to see where the moral high ground lies. But when ordinary people reason, "We can have 1,200 families working here…that's more important than five cougars and three grizzly bears," many of us begin to feel a little uneasy and wish that the issues weren't sometimes so complicated.

The final problem is the need for perpetual vigilance. In 1990, when California passed Proposition 117 banning cougar hunting except under special circumstances, it seemed that the cat had turned a corner. The unwelcome "lord of stealthy murder" now had protected status. But people age, times get tougher, and attitudes change. Six years later, Proposition 117 was challenged and was reaffirmed only after a close fight.

*Unless their mother is killed by hunters or by a male cougar, these 4-month-old kittens have a good chance of surviving to maturity. Hunting and trapping are the greatest causes of mortality in wild cats.*

112

*Coyotes and other canids take predictable routes through their territories, but not cats. Sometimes, they walk right down a trail. Sometimes, they're to one side of it. Sometimes, they're in the woods nearby. It's hard to predict which way they'll choose next. They're always exploring.*
　　　　　　　　　　　　　　　　　　　　　　　　—STEVE KNICK

Even protected areas are not the inviolate sanctuaries we may imagine. National parks suffer unrelenting pressure from developers. As management policies shift with the political winds, parks are eroded from the core and nibbled from the edges. And, unfortunately, in the war for wilderness, a battle won may be a battle won temporarily; but a battle lost is a battle lost forever.

There are no better examples of the fickleness of park protection than North America's two crown jewels: Yellowstone National Park in the United States and Banff National Park in Canada. In recent years, Yellowstone has become friendlier to all four-footed creatures, but it has a long and shabby history of "controlling" its carnivores to appease ranchers on the park's periphery. As for Banff, with its always cozy relationship between developers and the park brass, its new ski hill, its indoor mall and its divided superhighway ripping through prime wildlife habitat, Canadians should hang their heads in shame at the mere mention of the place.

Of the three cats, the bobcat seems to have the most secure future. Over the years, it has endured Texans who try to punch it out of trees, consumers who prefer it in the shape of fur coats and entrepreneurs who transform its homeland into gated communities. It remains the great survivor. It lives equally well in wilderness and in the shadow of farms and subdivisions. It doesn't kill children. It eats anything. It has the same bold temperament that allows the house sparrow, the coyote and the raccoon to flourish in our midst. I'll stake my money on the bobcat any day.

Just as adaptability protects the bobcat, inaccessibility of habitat currently safeguards the lynx. It is hard to say whether the coming millennium will largely transform the virgin timber of the great northland into industrial forest, but at least the distances are so vast and the season for building roads so short that over most of its range, the lynx is not immediately imperiled.

*It's sufficient just to know that sometimes, in the shadows of dusk, felines on huge paws still creep across the land.*

—GARY TURBAK

In the South, however, the lynx's fragile state becomes clear. Specialists do badly in a changing world, and with its one-note diet and timid ways, this northerner fares poorly in the fragmented forests of southern Canada and the Lower 48. Here, it is no longer the superbly adapted shadow cat of the snows but, rather, a sensitive species clinging to existence by one or two of its retractile claws. In New York's Adirondack Mountains, the lynx originally disappeared in the 1880s. An attempt in the early 1990s to reintroduce the lynx by importing 83 cats from the Yukon has not succeeded, owing mainly to car mortality and to the lynx's penchant to go on marathon walks to parts unknown. "If I had a dozen animals still out there," says project coordinator Rainer Brocke, "I'd be happy."

Cougars, like wolves and grizzly bears, may be more powerful on the surface than their smaller rivals, but they are also more vulnerable. We have already chased the cougar from the Atlantic shores through the Appalachians, the

*A tension-filled truce exists for a few days when two cougars come together to mate. Otherwise, cougars meet so rarely that they haven't evolved the submissive gestures to defuse aggression, as wolves have, and fights to the death are common.*

Great Lakes and the Prairies, until it now exists mainly in a few deserts and in the Rocky Mountains. Its need for land puts it in conflict with our need for land. It is too big and imposing to ignore or to pass undetected through the human gauntlet between habitable islands of wilderness.

Then there is the rare but emotional issue of some inept deer-slaying cougar killing the occasional bicyclist or child. Or the more regular traumatic abductions of a family pet. Even nature lovers who enjoy beautiful sunsets and hermit thrushes and quiet summer days by the lake don't always welcome the perilous presence of a "forest shark" in the neighborhood.

## ON COUGARS

*Any animal that eats sheep can't be all bad.*

—EDWARD ABBEY

Cougars, wolves and grizzly bears are the royalty of the North American wilderness, but it's uncertain whether in the long run, they will be able to survive outside of zoos and parks. One 1981 study concluded that even today in the new Northeast, with its regrown forests and comeback deer, conflicts with humans—mainly road-kill and hunting mortality—would prevent the successful return of the eastern cougar.

Yet it may still be possible to preserve enough wilderness for the great cats—without closing borders to immigration and offering a free transistor radio to every man who volunteers for a vasectomy, as family planners in India did some years ago. Researcher Paul Beier's work in southern California suggests that cougars will use relatively narrow forest corridors (450 yards wide) and even narrower road underpasses joining habitable areas. If we were to create a network of these corridors, the big cats could move freely from protected area to protected area. It would prevent the Florida panther syndrome, in which one small population is permanently isolated from other populations by an unbridgeable sea of development. The most ambitious plan calls for a "Paseo Pantera"—a continuous path of the panther—linking Patagonia to British Columbia in a long green necklace of parks and corridors.

You and I may never see a wild cat on our travels throughout North America, but we're immeasurably enriched by the possibility that one day, while clearing a ridge, we may glimpse a tawny shape with a ropy tail melting into the dark underbrush, away from us.

*As it steps into an uncertain future, even the versatile bobcat may face hard times. Our forest cats have shown that they can bounce back from trapping, hunting and cyclic food shortages. But whether these masters of secrecy can survive in an ever-shrinking wilderness is unknown.*

ACKNOWLEDGMENTS

Not only did Tom Kitchin and Vicki Hurst supply the magnificent photographs for this book, but our almost daily conversations about both text and pictures helped make this a true joint venture. Pierre Guevremont of First Light Associated Photographers got the project off the ground. Tracy Read, Susan Dickinson and Laurel Aziz of Bookmakers Press skillfully refined the raw text and handled the production, and Ulrike Bender of Studio Eye produced an elegant design. Together, our aim has been to leave you with a book that is as readable and accurate as it is a pleasure to look at.

Many researchers kindly shared their knowledge and their reminiscences with me and also read the manuscript for accuracy. In particular, I'd like to thank Ted Bailey, Paul Beier, Bill Berg, Duncan Bourne, Melanie Culver, Mark Ingstrom, Martin Jalkotzy, Doug Janz, Warren Johnson, Dennis Jordan, Steve Knick, Ken Logan, Kerry Murphy, Stephen O'Brien, Gerry Parker, Kim Poole, Melody Roelke, John Seidensticker, Bob Stephenson, Jay Tischendorf, Blaire Van Valkenburgh and Rick Ward. Ted Levin and Ross Morgan helped me sort out what is known about the eastern cougar in Vermont. Brian Slough was particularly patient with my endless E-mail questions about lynx. Kevin Seymour kept any quick assumptions I made about cats from fossilizing into final opinions. Finally, the late Knut Atkinson supplied helpful information about Vancouver Island cougars just days before he and two companions perished in a canoe mishap.

—*Jerry Kobalenko*

Many people helped us in making the photographs for this book. In particular, we would like to thank Hugh and Eleanore Oakes for introducing us to our first forest cats; Jean Stéphan Groulx and Pierre Guevremont for taking care of business; and Tom and Pat Leeson, Lynn Stone, Murray O'Neill and Larry and Zoie Tooze for their advice and companionship on the road. Most of all, we would like to thank our parents for their love and support through the years—the finest kind of encouragement a couple of kids could ask for.

—*Thomas Kitchin and Victoria Hurst*

**RECOMMENDED READING**

*America's Great Cats,* text by Gary Turbak, photographs by Alan Carey. Flagstaff: Northland Publishing, 1986. The most articulate and readable of all the popular photo/text books on cougars, bobcats and lynx. Thanks to the graceful style, the information flows across the page with the lightness of a cat.

*The Ben Lilly Legend,* J. Frank Dobie. Boston: Little, Brown and Company, 1950. The book has the flavor of one of today's unauthorized celebrity biographies, top-heavy with hearsay and yarn. Still, for anyone interested in old attitudes toward bears and cougars, Lilly is the most colorful practitioner of the pioneer art of wholesale slaughter.

*Bobcat Year,* Hope Ryden. New York: Lyons & Burford, 1981. Imagine putting minicams on a family of bobcats and observing their life for a year. That's what Ryden has set out to do in this fictional tale from a bobcat's-eye view, using a mixture of imagination and biology.

*Cougar, The American Lion,* Kevin Hansen. Flagstaff: Northland Publishing, 1992. Valuable mainly for its tables and its meticulous footnotes, which allow readers to track down more information on virtually every sentence. Despite the book's academic presentation, it avoids being too stuffy.

*The Ghost Walker,* R.D. Lawrence. Totem Books, 1984. An example of the cougar as spiritual quest, but Lawrence doesn't just worship the signs of its passing—he spends astonishing amounts of time with the big cat itself. More than once, he watches a wild cougar kill a deer—an experience that has eluded almost everyone else, including biologists who've studied the cats for 10 years. Other intimate moments are also unique. His writing is so good and his experiences so outstanding that it's unclear whether the book is documentary fact or autobiographical novel.

*Great Cats: Majestic Creatures of the Wild*, John Seidensticker and Susan Lumpkin, editors. London: Merehurst Limited, 1991. *The* reference book on wild cats of the world. As lavishly illustrated as a CD-ROM, but more in-depth. The list of authors is a who's who of the world's wild-cat researchers.

*Lives of the Game Animals, Volume 1*, Ernest Thompson Seton. Boston: Charles T. Brandford Company, 1953. Research today may be more precise, but you have to love 19th-century science, with its mixture of facts and charming personal tales. This is a classic of the genre. First published in 1909, it is a treasure trove of firsthand stories about cougars, bobcats and lynx. Seton's justifiably famous writing enlivens even the basic descriptions. Little wonder that in his field, he is quoted as often as Shakespeare.

*Mountain Lion: An Unnatural History of Pumas and People*, Chris Bolgiano. Mechanicsburg, Pennsylvania: Stackpole Books, 1995. The personal experience rambles a bit, but this is still a useful and up-to-date guide to native, pioneer and modern attitudes about cougars, cougar attacks, cougar politics and eastern cougar questions.

*The Natural History of Cats*, Claire Necker. New York: Delta Books, 1977. One of two fine books about domestic cats that will also appeal to wild-cat lovers. Necker draws on a seemingly inexhaustible fund of literary quotes, fables and assorted stories about cats yet tempers the pure entertainment with several fascinating chapters on cat senses and biology.

*The Puma: Legendary Lion of the Americas*, Jim Bob Tinsley. El Paso, Texas: Western Press, 1987. A well-known country singer of generations past, Tinsley squirreled away historical tidbits on the cougar for 30 years. The result is a book full of interesting trivia, plus archival black-and-white photos from a hunter's point of view.

*The Puma: Mysterious American Cat*, Stanley Young & Edward Goldman. Washington, D.C.: The American Wildlife Institute, 1946. This classic work is so enduring that it is still commonly referenced in such sober venues as *The Journal of Mammalogy*. But writer Barry Lopez warns that "the works of Stanley Young so earnestly mix fact and fiction," they should not be taken for science.

*Swamp Screamer*, Charles Fergus. New York: North Point Press, 1996. No pictures, but it's the best-written of all the big-cats books, full of dry humor and fascinating tidbits on the Florida panther and cougars generally. Fergus's unspoken theme is that it's impossible to tell the Florida panther's story without writing about the human players— hence his brief but revealing sketches of all the biologists, conservationists and administrators he meets. When a novelist like Fergus takes up a nonfiction labor of love, the result is miles beyond most professional journalism.

*The Tiger in the House*, Carl Van Vechten. New York: Alfred A. Knopf, 1968. First published in 1920, this is still the most erudite book on cats ever written. Although it's about domestic felines rather than wild ones, it's well worth the read—especially if you believe, as Ernest Thompson Seton did, that a cougar is just a house cat multiplied by 20.

*The Tribe of Tiger*, Elizabeth Marshall Thomas. New York: Simon & Schuster, 1994. An observant naturalist ponders the nature of felines. Thomas comes up with some nice insights and supports her case with many personal anecdotes, especially from her time with lions in the Kalahari during the 1950s.

**INTERNET SITES**     As any Internet user knows, Web sites are born, die and change location every day, but as of mid-1997, these are the best places in cyberspace to learn more about cougars, bobcats and lynx.

*Index of cat links*:
http://www.cathouse-fcc.org/links.html
Lists most of the following sites and many more. Includes foreign big cats.

*Big Cats OnLine*:
http://dialspace.dial.pipex.com/agarman/
and
*The Cyber Zoomobile*:
http://www.primenet.com/~brendel/
Two good school or general references on the big cats.

*Bigger Big Cats Page*:
http://www.lam.mus.ca.us/~pcannon/cats.html
Informative sketches on all the world's wild cats, from the 2-pound rusty spotted cat to the 800-pound tiger.

*European lynx*:
http://lynx.uio.no/jon/lynx/
Deals mainly with the European lynx in Norway, where it is hunted and possibly endangered.

*Florida Panther Society*:
http://supernet.net/~chrisd/panther.html
The most in-depth of all the cat sites, with background information, newspaper articles, even a life history of each Florida panther under study.

**rec.animals.wildlife**
The newsgroup for debates about the latest cougar attack and other hot wildlife topics. Like everywhere on the Net,

it draws a mixture of lonely people, inveterate chatterers and a few knowledgeable sources that make it worthwhile.

*Search engine for newsgroup topics*:
http://www.dejanews.com/forms/dnq.html
Type "cougar or lynx or bobcat or panther" in the query line provided to call up every recent newsgroup posting about these animals. Predictably, there are a lot of entries from **rec.animals.wildlife** and **talk.environment** but also from unexpected sources such as **rec.bicycles**. Note: Since these cat names also refer to sports teams and even Internet software, your search will call up a huge number of entries. Fortunately, most of the genuine feline references are at the beginning of the list.

Ambush hunting, 50
Attacks on humans by cougars, 84-89
  how to handle, 87
  on Vancouver Island, B.C., 89
Audubon, John James, 30
Banff National Park, 113
Beier, Paul, 87, 117
Bibliography, 119-121
Black coloration in wild cats, 103
*Bobcat of North America, The*, by Stanley Young, 30
Bobcats (*Lynx rufus*), 22-30; photos, 6, 23, 26, 28-29, 49, 62, 64-65, 67, 81, 90, 116
  and fur industry, 25
  comparison with lynx, 22-24
  cycle with blacktailed jackrabbit, 62
  diet, 62-63
  elusiveness, 26-27
  family life, 74
  farm stock as prey, 66
  feet, 24
  fighting, 27-30; photo, 25
  fighting with coyote, photo, 76
  future, 113
  hunting technique, 63-66
  in native mythology, 80, 90
  jumping abilities, 44
  kittens, 74; photos, 69, 70
  mating, 71
  mating call, 75
  origin and history, 44-45
  physical characteristics, 22, 26
  population density, 26
  range, 24, 26; map, 24
  range, individual, 27
  relationship to lions and tigers, 43
  running speed, 44
  statistics (chart), 27
  study of, 24-25
  success of species, 22
  tail, photo, 46
  temperament, 30
  territory, 27
  trapping of, 25
*Book of the Damned, The*, by Charles Fort, 106
Breeding season, 71-74
Burroughs, John, 74
Cabeza de Vaca, Alvar Nuñez, 83

Cats. See also Bobcats; Cougars; Eastern cougar; Florida panther; Lynx
  ability to kill instantly, 53
  attacks on humans, 84-89
  black coloration, 103
  DNA research, 43
  eating habits, 50
  European (*Lynx lynx*), 44
  evolution and classification, 38-41, 43
  future, threats to, 110-117
  geographical origin, 43-44
  human attempts to eliminate, 83-84
  hunting, 48-66
  in native mythology, 80-83, 90, 91
  jumping abilities compared with humans', 44
  killing bite, 53
  names used for places, 89
  physical characteristics, 46-47
  relations with canines, 76
  relations with humans, 80-89
  reproduction, 68-78
  running speed compared with humans', 44
  saber-toothed, 40
  similarities of different species, 38-40
  specialization as predators, 38
Cheetah, relationship to cougars, 43
Classification of cats, 43
  difficulty of determining, 38-41, 45
Claws, cats', 47, 50
Collarbone, cats', 47
Cougars (*Puma concolor*), 8-22; photos, 5, 9, 18-19, 20, 42, 51, 52, 85, 86, 88, 101, 102, 104-105, 107, 108, 114, 115. See also Florida panther
  attacks on humans, 84-89
  attacks on humans, how to handle, 87
  attacks on humans, Vancouver Island, B.C., 89
  bounty hunting, 83-84
  breeding season, 71-74
  diet, 53
  early adulthood, 78
  early European mentions, 83

eastern (*Puma concolor couguar*), 99-109

eastern, and "black panther" sightings, 106

eastern, and deer population, 100-103

eastern, evidence for existence, 103-106

eastern, habitat loss, 100-103

eastern, question of existence, 99-109

eastern, released pets responsible for sightings, 107-109

eastern, sightings, explanations, 106-109

eating habits, 50

elusiveness, 8

farm stock as prey, 56

fighting, 21-22

future, 115-117

grooming, photo, 10

habitat, 14

hunting abilities, 52-54; photo, 55

in native mythology, 80-82, 83

jumping abilities, 44

kittens, 77-78; photos, 16, 71, 72-73, 77, 79, 112

mating, 71

mating call, 74-75

names, 8-10

origin and history, 40, 44

parenting, 68, 78

paw print, photo, 21

physical characteristics, 10, 11-12, 54

population, 12

population density, 17

range, 12-14; map, 12

range, individual, 14, 17

relationship to cheetah, 43

running, photo, 13

running speed, 44

statistics (chart), 11

study of, 14-21

swimming, photo, 15

tail, photo, 47

teeth, photo, 46

territoriality, 15-17, 21-22

Texas subspecies (*Puma concolor stanleyana*), 98

tracking of, 14-15

Courtship, 68

Coyote and bobcat fighting,

photo, 76

Cycles, predator-prey, 56-60, 62, 75

Deer

mule, overpopulation when predators eliminated, 54-55

population and eastern cougar, 100-103

DNA research on cats, 43

Dobie, J. Frank, 84

Dogs, relationship with cats, 76

Duffett, Boyd, 37

Ears and hearing, cats', 46

Eastern cougar (*Puma concolor couguar*), 99-109

and "black panther" sightings, 106

and deer population, 100-103

evidence for existence, 103-106

habitat loss, 100-103

question of existence, 99-109

released pets responsible for sightings, 107-109

sightings, explanations, 106-109

Eating habits of cats, 50

Evolution of cats, 43

difficulty of determining, 38-40, 45

Eyes, cats', 46

Fakahatchee Strand, Florida, 94-96

Family life, 74

Feast-or-famine eating habits, 50

Florida panther (*Puma concolor coryi*), 12, 92-99; photos, 93, 95

crossbreeding, 98-99

future, 99

habitat loss, 92, 96

inbreeding, 94, 96-97

range map, 97

Florida swamps, 94-96

Flushing prey, 50-51

Fort, Charles, *The Book of the Damned*, 106

Fur industry and bobcats, 25

Geographical origin of cats, 43-44

Goff, John, 80

Gums, cats', 47

Habitat loss as threat to existence of wild cats, 110-113

Hare, snowshoe

as lynx's chief prey, 37

cycle with lynx, 56-60, 75
Heart, cats', 46
Heels, cats', 47
Hornocker, Maurice, 15-17, 52, 89
Humans, relations with wild cats, 80-99
Hunting, 48-66
    accidents, 51-52
    techniques, 50-51
Hurst, Vicki, 26-27
Information sources, 119-123
Internet sites, 122-123
Jackrabbit, blacktailed, cycle with bobcat, 62
Jalkotzy, Martin, 8, 14-15, 68, 78
Jodouin, Jim, 99
Kaibab Plateau, elimination of predators, 54
Killing bite, 53
Kitchin, Tom, 26-27, 75
Knick, Steve, 62, 74
Lawson, John, 80
Laycock, George, 54
Legs, cats', 47
Levin, Ted, 109
Lilly, Ben, 83-84
Lions
    African, hunting success compared with cougars', 52
    American, 40
    mountain, 10. See also Cougars
    relationship to bobcats and lynx, 43
Locomotion, cats', 47
Logan, Ken, 17-21, 82
*Lynx*
    *canadensis*, 30-37. See also Lynx
    *lynx*, 44
    *rufus*, 22-30. See also Bobcats
Lynx (*Lynx canadensis*), 30-37; photos, 31, 32, 36, 37, 57, 58, 59, 61, 91, 111
    attacks on humans, 37
    breeding season, 71
    comparison with bobcats, 22-24
    cycle (chart), 58-60
    cycle with snowshoe hare, 56-60, 75
    diet, 22, 34, 37, 60
    eating habits, 50

family life, 74
feet, 24, 32-33; photo, 41
fighting, photo, 25
future, 113-115
habitat, 34, 35
hunting, 33
hunting, cooperative, 75-77
hunting technique, 50-51, 60
in native mythology, 80, 82-83, 91
jumping abilities, 44
kittens, photos, 74, 75
mating call, 74, 75
origin and history, 44-45
physical characteristics, 22, 32
range, 24, 30; map, 34
range, individual, 35-37
relationship to lions and tigers, 43
reproduction and cycle with snowshoe hare, 75
running, photo, 35, 40
running speed, 44
size, 30-32
sleeping, 34
statistics (chart), 33
swimming, 35
tail, photo, 46
temperament, 30, 34
territory, 35-37
Maps, range
    bobcat, 24
    cougar, 12
    Florida panther, 97
    lynx, 34
Mating, 71
    calls, 74-75
Morton, Thomas, 22
Mythology of cats, 80-83
    bobcats, 90
    cougars, 83
    lynx, 91
Names, wild cats' as place names, 89
Names for cougars, 8-10
National Cancer Institute, 41-43
Newsgroups, 122-123
O'Brien, Stephen, 41-43, 97
Panthers, 10. See also Cougars
    Florida (*Puma concolor coryi*), 12, 92-99; photos, 93, 95
    Florida, crossbreeding, 98-99
    Florida, future, 99

Florida, habitat loss, 92, 96
Florida, inbreeding, 94, 96-97
Florida, range map, 97
Parenting, 68
Parker, Gerry, 24, 106
Places named after wild cats, 89
Poole, Kim, 60, 77
Predator-prey relationships
    balance of nature, 54-55
    cycles, 56-60, 62, 75
Predators, mistaken assumptions
    about, 54-55
*Proailurus*, 40
*Puma concolor*, 8-22. See also
    Cougars
        *coryi*, 92-99. See also Florida
            panther
        *couguar*, 99-109. See also
            Eastern cougar
        *stanleyana*, 98
Pumas, 10. See also Cougars
Rabbit, jack-, blacktailed, and
    cycle with bobcat, 62
Radio-collars, 17
Range maps
    bobcat, 24
    cougar, 12
    Florida panther, 97
    lynx, 34
Reading list, 119-121
Reproduction, 68-78
Roelke, Melody, 94, 97
Saber-toothed cat, 40
Seidensticker, John, 17, 50, 53,
    87-88
Seton, Ernest Thompson, 11, 34
Seymour, Kevin, 38
Similarities of different cat species,
    38-40
Skin, cats', 46
Slough, Brian, 77
Sources of information, 119-123
Specialization of cats, 38
Spine, cats', 46
Stalking, 50
Sutherland, Bob, 78
Swamps, Florida, 94-96
Sweanor, Linda, 17-21, 82
Tail, cats', 47
Tanner, Philip, 85
Teeth, cats', 46-47
Texas cougar (*Puma concolor
    stanleyana*), 98
Tigers, relationship to bobcats and

lynx, 43
Tongue, cats', photo, 57
Van Valkenburgh, Blaire, 45
Vancouver Island, B.C., cougar
    attacks on humans, 89
Veitch, Alasdair, 33
Vespucci, Amerigo, 83
Web sites, 122
Whiskers, cats', 46
Wiles, Wilbur, 15-17
Yellowstone National Park, 113
Young, Stanley, *The Bobcat of
    North America*, 30